The Still Center

The Still Center

A Philosophy for Our Time

Burton Porter

Algora Publishing
New York

Library of Congress Cataloging-in-Publication Data

Names: Porter, Burton F., author.
Title: The still center: a philosophy for our time / Burton Porter.
Description: New York: Algora Publishing, [2021] | Summary: "Prof. Burton
    Porter surveys philosophy and ethics in a clear, concise way, examines
    our present attitudes and values, and offers signposts for a successful
    life. With full, 21st century awareness, the author points to dimensions
    of human beings that can be realized to create a fulfilling existence"—
    Provided by publisher.
Identifiers: LCCN 2021042802 (print) | LCCN 2021042803 (ebook) | ISBN
    9781628944792 (trade paperback) | ISBN 9781628944808 (hardcover) |
    ISBN 9781628944815 (pdf)
Subjects: LCSH: Ethics, Modern—21st century. | Civilization, Modern—
    21st century—Moral and ethical aspects. | Life.
Classification: LCC BJ320 .P665 2021 (print) | LCC BJ320 (ebook) | DDC
    170—dc23
LC record available at https://lccn.loc.gov/2021042802
LC ebook record available at https://lccn.loc.gov/2021042803

Printed in the United States

To Barbara,
Whom I cherish
Up to the sun, the moon
And the stars

Things fall apart; the center cannot hold;
Mere anarchy is loosed upon the world,
The blood-dimmed tide is loosed, and everywhere
The ceremony of innocence is drowned;
The best lack all conviction, while the worst
Are full of passionate intensity.

—W. B. Yeats

TABLE OF CONTENTS

1. Our Age of Science and Technology

It will not come as a surprise that people today think of the world as physical, not spiritual, somewhat modified by deference to religion but as natural, without a supernatural dimension. The managers of life insurance companies do not give lower rates to people who pray. Rather, they make business decisions, setting their rates in accordance with actuarial tables, assessing the risk. Fewer people are going to church on Sunday, and those who do are practical on weekdays, which means they are oriented toward worldly goals. What's more, they don't seem more generous or merciful in their business dealings because of the service or the sermon. Slash and burn, and scorched earth, will take you further in business than being likeable. Nice guys finish last; take no prisoners.

Few people now think it is sinful to accumulate money, that they will not get into heaven any more than a camel can pass through the eye of a needle. Churches welcome the rich, who are often distinguished members of the congregation, and wealth and worship go hand in hand. Financial success is life's report card, and the afterlife is a remote possibility.

In our present age, the material world is what matters to us, sometimes all that matters, and we rely on science in order to know that world, and technology to get things done. To most people what counts as evidence is experiments, studies, and surveys, and we trust statistics, metrics, and algorithms for verification. Intuitions are not credited; neither are premonitions, or private revelations. Subjective certainty is thought to vary inversely with objective certainty, and the objective kind is based on empirical facts. Nothing besides matter is real, and the basic unit of that reality is the atom with its protons, neutrons, and electrons, indivisible and immutable. Elementary particles have taken the place of spirits and deities.

Communism and capitalism seem to join hands in this, believing that the physical world is the basic world. In Marxist theory it is the foundation on which the superstructure is built — a superstructure that includes law, politics, religion, war, social class, the arts, and (dialectical) history. The Russian, Chinese, and American revolutions all reached their apogee in enormous material production. Through an intellectual sleight-of-hand, capitalism was made compatible with Christianity, while communist countries see religious faith and economic development as alternatives, an either/or.

This material reality is thought accessible by our senses, filtered by science, mainly seeing (80%), but also hearing, touching, smelling, and tasting. The sense organs, along with the brain and nervous system, allow us to perceive the external world, and we augment them with extra-neural instruments such as microscopes, and telescopes. Sometimes biologists will also refer to a sense of location, being aware of where our body is situated: we know our right hand from our left hand, even in the dark. But science does not acknowledge a "sixth sense" of precognition or telepathy, or any inner, incommunicable truths. If it cannot be expressed, there may not be anything to express. Having the senses continually transmitting data, means we are conscious, and it separates the living from the dead.

One problem, of course, is that if we claim that reality is only what is scientifically testable, that claim itself is not testable, and cannot be called true...

***

We inhabit a physical world in another way — in our consumer culture that equates living well with owning property and tangible goods, eating high-end food and vacationing in exotic locations. You must also be invested in the Stock Market and have a diversified portfolio. According to Thomas Picketty and other economists, wealth from stocks and bonds exceeds that of salaries today.

Everything we possess contributes to our sense of self-worth, as well as impressing others, especially a late model car, clothes in the latest fashion, our children in private school, and owning a large house in a prosperous zip code. And there must be a zoning ordinance of so many acres, with any changes in the design approved by the neighborhood association. It is what Thorstein Veblen called "conspicuous consumption," and it sends a message to ourselves and others that we have arrived, we have won. In the United States, a person's value is determined by how much he is worth.

If you do not own very much, then you have not fulfilled the American dream and are unimportant. Wealth determines class, status, and social position, much more than family background. In Europe, the impoverished lord still has high status, but in this country, poverty is an embarrassment. People here have so many possessions that they need to rent storage facilities because their houses cannot contain it all. Our attics and basements are stuffed, not just because some things have sentimental value but because having more makes us feel bigger. And we consume so much food that being overweight is a national health problem, and dieting a national obsession. Some of our resistance to losing weight comes from the feeling that being smaller means being less. In the world at large, 9 million people die of hunger and malnutrition every year, including 3.1 million children, but the developed countries have a surplus of food, overflowing markets, and a waste disposal problem. A garbage can in New York City eats better than half the world's population.

Materialism is part of our worldview — that physical things matter, and little else does. Corporation executives command the greatest respect because they receive the highest salaries, and own the most possessions. For vacations they go to Cancun or St. Barth, and enjoy the tropical breezes, lying in a hammock on a beach, a mimosa in their hand, and a trophy wife beside them. That is seen as the good life, of prosperity, leisure, and relaxation, earned in the marketplace, envied by everyone else. If you can travel to places with sun and sand, enjoying physical pleasures, then you are living the good life.

Because of our life style, Americans pollute the air, land, and water per capita more than any other nation, and that, of course, accelerates climate change. We maintain our standard of living at the world's expense. Economic development and environmental protection are always at loggerheads, and the developers usually win.

Beneath it all is a common assumption that acquiring more of the earth's goods means a better life. Financial prosperity is essential, and producing and consuming are our basic activities. In another age, William Wordsworth said, "The world is too much with us; late and soon,/ Getting and spending we lay waste our powers." That warning might well apply to our own time. We live in an age where getting and spending is the pattern of our lives, an age when the physical aspect of life is most important, and by extension, the more objects we possess, the more important we become. We identify with what we own, and it makes us feel like more.

In any case, they are now part of the (air-conditioned) air we breathe. Our labor-saving products and techniques, such as motor vehicles, airplanes, and ships, washing machines, refrigerators, and stoves, plumbing, electricity, and heating, raise us above the subsistence level. Animals spend most of their time looking for food, whereas people today have been freed from continuous hunting, gathering, and farming, and have the leisure to enjoy their time on earth. Thanks to science and technology, along with our natural bipedalism, opposable thumb and forefinger, and complex brain, human beings can create art, music, and literature, and reflect on life in the process of living it. Tool-using and tool-making are not unique to human beings, but we are scarcely human without that ability.

***

However, life may be wider than the material or physical. Perhaps one of the greatest dangers of science and technology is that it will reduce human existence to nothing but matter in motion. Science frees us to create art objects, as well as political, ethical, and religious systems, but they are then disprized compared to the hard-nosed, physical world we live in. "All the secrets of the universe are written in mathematics," the scientist says, and this translates to the belief that everything real can be quantified.

This viewpoint excludes values and meaning from life, leaving us in a state of bewilderment as to our purpose in being. Amorality and pragmatism rule, a utilitarian calculation of benefit and loss, rendered in terms of improvement or deterioration in our standard of living. But this leaves us without a compass; the ship lacks direction, and is taking on water. Religion offers a solution to our confusion, and allays our existential anxieties, but at the expense of our Enlightenment understanding. Prayer does not seem to help because we're not sure anyone is listening, and our prayers do not come true at a rate higher than chance. We are left in a state of spiritual and moral nihilism.

This reductionism can best be seen in the popular, psychological theory of Behaviorism that dismisses the idea of the mind as "a ghost in the machine," denies free will, and treats people as stimulus-response mechanisms. Psychology is considered the study of behavior, not of the mind, and by reducing people to this level, the behaviorist can make it work. The strongest stimulus always wins, whether in child rearing, advertising, prison rehabilitation, athletics, employee motivation, or education — the last considered job training. (There is something circular, however, in identifying the strongest stimulus as the one that wins.) Rewards are better than punishments, but both are effective.

The principal figurers in behaviorism are Ivan Pavlov, the 19th century originator, and B. F. Skinner, the 20th century popularizer who laid out the principles that are in use today. Skinner's books, *Science and Human Behavior*, and *Beyond Freedom and Dignity*, have been especially influential, as well as his novel *Walden II*. Aldous Huxley's *Brave New World* and Thomas Pynchon's *Gravity's Rainbow* are both based on behaviorist principles.

In a well-known experiment, Pavlov rang a bell (or used a whistle or electric shock) to signal the arrival of food to a dog. The dog began salivating when it heard the bell, associating the sound with eating. Salivating was its response to the stimulus of the bell, in advance of the appearance of food. The dog had been "conditioned" by stimuli, the events in the environment, and its responses were the observable behavior.

Skinner has been particularly anxious that operant conditioning be employed in social engineering. To Skinner's mind, everyone's actions are conditioned, and the choice is whether to control that conditioning for human good, or to let it operate in a random manner, as it does today.

He was anxious for psychology to be based on experimentation and gain respectability as a science. He dismissed earlier psychologists, such as Sigmund Freud, because their theories relied on anecdotal evidence — in Freud's case, the clinical disclosures of his patients in psychotherapy. Freud was also criticized because his reference group was not stratified, and that is unscientific. All his patients were repressed, middle class, Viennese women who, once they learned his system, began dreaming in Freudian symbols. This was self-reinforcing, and contaminated the findings. Feminists later criticized Freud for his idea of "penis envy," the Oedipus and Electra complex, and for asking, "What do women want?"

Various schools of psychology have criticized behaviorism for treating the symptoms, not the cause. You can change people's conduct but you haven't reached the root of their disorder. Cognitive psychology, Functionalism, Gestalt, and Humanism have all challenged Behaviorism for, among other things, overlooking the mind. But in our times, the use of trials, tests, measurements, and questionnaires validate a theory. Behaviorism is on the rise, probably because it deals with observable conduct, and keys into our concept of reality as physical. We accept the existence of the brain, but the mind is too close to the notion of a soul and can't be detected by evidence-based science. It cannot be characterized or quantified by chemical analysis.

The philosophic movement of Logical Positivism has been especially influential in furthering this empirical view. Its chief proponent was A. J. Ayer in the 20th century, a colorful, English philosopher, flamboyant and humorous, called "the wickedest man at Oxford." His book *Language, Truth and Logic* popularized the Positivist position: "I call a sentence meaningful," he writes, "if and only if, we are able to specify the operations which would confirm it as being true, or reject it as being false." Ayer labeled this the "Verification Principle."

For example, the statement 'The cat is on the mat' is meaningful because we can prove or disprove the assertion by our senses. If we see a certain shape, hear a certain sound, and feel a certain texture, that proves the cat is on the mat. The same rule applies to 'Ice melts at 32 degrees,' 'Giraffes are taller than zebras,' and 'Diamonds are hard.' These statements all qualify as meaningful because they can be empirically tested. However, the same is not true of 'The music of Bartok is purple,' 'There are angels in heaven,' or 'People should be considered innocent until proven guilty.' These sentences seem to make sense because of their grammatical structure, but they are actually nonsense.

It would be the same as saying, as Lewis Carroll did in "The Jabberwocky," 'Twas brillig and the slithy toves/ Did gyre ang gimble in the wabe,/ All mimsy were the borogroves,/ And the mome raths outgrabe.' This passage has the appearance of being meaningful but is in fact absurd; it masquerades as something sensible because of its grammatical structure. In other words, it is only when a sentence can be tested by the senses that it can be called meaningful. The logical positivists are not saying that non-testable propositions are false, but much worse: that they have no meaning.

Wielding the Verification Principle, A. J. Ayer and the Positivists dismissed as nonsense all ethical, religious, aesthetic, and political claims. Otto Spengler, the 20th century German historian wrote, "The color of philosophy is brown"; the poet Shelley wrote, "Life like a dome of many-colored glass, stains the white radiance of eternity"; and the 19th century philosopher G. W. F. Hegel wrote. "The Absolute enters into but is itself incapable of evolution and progress." These sentences seem to make sense, but what evidence is relevant to their truth or falsity? Since nothing could count for or against them, they are actually senseless, and to ask if they are correct or incorrect is an inappropriate question.

To take ethics in particular, Ayer wrote, "The presence of an ethical symbol in a proposition adds nothing to its factual content. Thus, if I say to someone, 'You acted wrongly in stealing that money,', I am not stating anything more than if I had simply said, 'You stole that money,' In adding that this action is wrong, I am not making any further statement about it. I am simply evincing my moral disapproval of it. It is as if I had said, 'You stole that money,' in a peculiar tone of horror, or written it with the addition of some special exclamation marks... If now I generalize my previous statement and say, 'Stealing is wrong,' I produce a sentence that has no factual meaning — that is, expresses no proposition that can be either true or false...I am merely expressing certain moral sentiments." Some commentators have called this the "boo-hurrah theory." In the above example, we are simply saying 'Hurrah for honesty, boo to dishonesty.' Ethical judgments simply express attitudes and vent feelings, but they aren't about any actions themselves.

Since its inception, this theory has permeated a great deal of contemporary thought, even though it was seriously challenged in its time. For example, it was pointed out that the Verification Principle itself couldn't pass the test of the Verification Principle, and should be declared meaningless. Some critics also argued that a statement can make sense even if it cannot be proven true or false. 'The king of France is bald' is meaningful, even if there is no present king of France, much less a bald one. This means that sentences can be meaningful on various levels, and need not be supported by empirical proof alone. Still others said that too much was being excluded that was worth saying. Kindness does seem better than cruelty, even if there is no scientific evidence to prove it.

Are Behaviorism and Logical Positivism like the person who thinks he has lost his keys on a dark road, and walks to a streetlight to look for them? Is life wider than the world accessible to science, and are physical objects the whole of reality, or only a dimension of it?

Of course, the danger in being open-minded is that it could allow all sorts of bizarre claims equal validity. Maybe there are zombies and vampires, ghosts, aliens, and Yetis, understood in a different way. But we do have reason as a filter to separate good sense from nonsense. For one thing, we have a basic rule of logic called "the law of non-contradiction." People cannot claim there are zombies and vampires, and that there aren't zombies and vampires. Contradictory propositions cannot both be true at the same time and in the same way. If a statement is true, then the opposite must be false. For example, if I say a tree is real, I cannot also claim the tree is not real. And a self-contradiction is not a mystery or a paradox for the expression of a higher truth, but simply absurd.

Also, reason dictates that we should take all the relevant factors into account, and provide the best interpretation of human experience. Logic can filter out the ridiculous claims, leaving a residue of the plausible.

Later in the book we will explore the ramifications of using reason in judging truth, but the point here is that the material world may not exhaust the whole of reality, and this position does not mean that every fanciful belief might well be true. We must be rational, but that rationality could be compatible with a more inclusive view of reality. Maybe the world is wider than what science can measure.

2. Body and Soul, Heaven and Earth

We think of ourselves as our bodies, the face that looks back at us in the mirror, the muscles we exercise, the skin that envelopes flesh and bones. In the Middle Ages it was the soul that constituted the essence of the person. Medicine was suspect, and doctors might even be the instruments of the devil. In any case, they treated just the physical disease. If people were sick, they would only recover if the soul were cured; treating the body would never redeem the soul. By extension, holy relics might help cure ailments -the bones of saints, a hair of a martyr, charms, amulets, and exorcisms, but not solely the remedies of physicians. Besides, we were meant to suffer on earth as penance for original sin, so doctors were interfering with God's will.

Medicine was permitted to some extent, especially if accompanied by the prayers of a priest. But in treating patients, physicians had to follow the classic Greek texts, which pivoted round the four "humors." These bodily fluids determined a person's health: blood, phlegm, black bile, and yellow bile. Each was associated with basic elements of earth, air, fire, and water, the four ages of infancy, adolescence, adulthood, and old age, the four gospels, the signs of the Zodiac, and even the directions of the compass. Good health consists in keeping our bodily fluids in harmony, and one's personality reflected whether there is an imbalance among the humors. The predominance of blood meant a cheerful, optimistic, confident disposition (sanguine); phlegm was associated with a calm, apathetic, unemotional personality (phlegmatic); black bile meant melancholy, gloom, despondency; a preponderance of yellow bile resulted in irritability, anger, a choleric attitude toward life (bilious).

To restore a patient's equilibrium, physicians had to balance a person's humors by various means. For instance, different foods that were cold, hot, wet or dry regulated a person's body. Warm pasta cleaned the stomach lining; barley soup was good for humid intestines; roses, which are cold and dry, would reduce inflammation of the brain. Contact with sacred waters was also restorative, whether fountains, rivers, fonts, or spas. Also essential was the use of signatures — cures for diseases marked in nature by God. For example, the red juices of bloodroot are good for the blood; the yellow fluid of celandine cures jaundice; eyebright with its oval spot cures eye diseases; and the sinuous shape of bugloss can be used to treat snakebites.

For centuries, bloodletting (phlebotomy) was a related cure that was thought to have a general positive effect. By choosing the proper vein, releasing or restricting blood flow, physicians could control the humors. In actuality, blood-letting often resulted in infection, a severed nerve or artery, and uncontrollable bleeding. Usually patients just grew weaker, or they simply died. Bloodletting, in fact, was one of the most harmful practices in the history of medicine. Today, doctors have adopted the reverse procedure of blood transfusions.

Although medicine was practiced, under the careful supervision of the church, doctors were generally identified with infernal sorcerers, practicing the unearthly magic of satanic cults. A popular proverb said, "Where there are three physicians, there are two atheists."

Medicine and surgery were carefully distinguished: physicians dealt with internal problems, surgeons treated wounds, fractures, skin diseases, etc. Because of a religious injunction against "shedding blood" (with the exception of blood-letting), surgeons were severely limited. They were only allowed to amputate limbs on battlefield, although the anesthetic potions that were used, hemlock juice, opium, and henbane, often proved fatal.

The dissection of cadavers was considered especially sinful, because it showed disrespect for the dead and for the body, which was the temple of the soul. The remains of the dead had to be smuggled in to doctors in basement laboratories, and there were severe penalties for grave robbing. Dissection was also prohibited because it revealed one of the divine mysteries: how the body was made. That was for God alone to know. It was even feared that both sexes would be found to have an equal number of ribs; since the creation of Eve, men should have one less. Vesalius created a controversy in 1543 when he suggested that men and women had the same number of ribs.

Medicine has now won the battle as people see themselves in physical terms. We dissect cadavers in medical schools, conduct autopsies, harvest organs, routinely perform transplants and use artificial body parts. The fact that hospitals are named St. Francis or St. Mary's shows the hostility between medicine and religion has come to an end. Sometimes there are minor skirmishes, for example between faith healing and medical practice, and Pentecostals still pray for their child's recovery rather than seek treatment at a doctor's office or hospital.

Mental illness (madness) was regarded by Medieval theologians as due to Satanic influence; people were "fiend-sick," and spiritual measures were needed to restore their souls. Sometimes these measures were humane: holy water, sacred relics, the breath of priests, visiting holy sites, drinking potions from church bells. The first step was to attack Satan's pride, which was his dominant characteristic. Obscene curses, vile insult should be hurled at him so he would leave the body of the "lunatic." Books of exorcisms contained hundreds of imprecations calling Satan a mangy beast, filthy sow, loathsome cobbler, envious crocodile, malodorous drudge, swollen toad, perfidious boar, greedy wolf, entangled spider, bestial drunkard, lustful and stupid one, and so forth. Thunder-words might also frighten Satan away, for example, "Schemhamphora," "Athanatos," "Tetragrammaton," and "Eheye."

Gradually, however, inhumane measures were used. The church accepted the notion that the indwelling demon had to be punished, which meant torture of the "madman." The point was to exorcize the devil, and the devil's power was such that gentle treatment might not be enough. This idea opened the door to the cruelest acts of the Middle Ages and some of the saddest chapters in religious history. Satan was being punished but it was the lunatic's body that was tortured. Flogging, hanging, ducking, pressing, the thumbscrew, the rack, the garrote, the wheel, the iron maiden — all were used on the insane. According to one report, the Jesuits in Vienna exorcized 12,652 devils in the year 1583. The specific justification cited was that Christ cast out demons and drove them into a herd of swine.

The same methods were used against heretics. Anyone accused of heresy, was tortured until they confessed, and everyone eventually confessed. Because blood should not be spilled, people's joints and bones were cracked instead. This practice went on for several hundred years.

Belief in demons flourished throughout the Middle Ages, which can be seen in Gothic cathedrals where there are representations of Satan and his hideous fiends, scourging people, poking them with tridents, dragging them to hell in chains. Carved gargoyles were placed at the cathedral corners and as downspouts of gutters. They are grotesques, but benevolent ones, designed to frighten off evil spirits. They have been described as "sermons in stone," teaching the illiterate that the Devil is never far away. Stained glass windows also depicted demons and monsters; one window in Chartres cathedral shows the exorcism of an insane man, a horned and hoofed hobgoblin spewing out from his mouth. Demonic possession is still part of Catholic doctrine, and exorcism is prescribed in cases of profuse blasphemy, speaking in tongues, supernatural abilities, knowledge of hidden things, and an aversion to anything holy.

So much pain and misery could have been avoided during the Middle Ages if doctors had been allowed to apply scientific knowledge to illness. Because of dogmatic beliefs, thousands of people suffered terribly from curable diseases or were needlessly tortured as a consequence of ignorance. Gradually, medical treatment has come to be judged consistent with God's will, and health a divine blessing.

***

Science also clashed with religion over *cosmology* or the structure of the universe. Medieval theologians believed the theory of a monk named Cosmas who, in *Christian Topography*, declared that the earth is a flat rectangle, perhaps a disk, surrounded by four seas. Its dimensions are four hundred days' journey long, two hundred days wide, and the four corners of the earth symbolize the four seasons and the twelve months of the year. Gigantic walls enclose the land and seas, and rise to support "the pillars of heaven." Two levels make up this oblong box, divided by the solid vault of the heavens: the lower one stretches from the earth to the stars and contains human life; the upper one is the home of divine beings, including angels who carry out God's work. "We say therefore with Isaiah that the heaven embracing the earth is a vault, with Job that it is joined to the earth, and with Moses that the length of the earth is greater than its breadth."

There were further descriptions concerning the next world. A hell exists below the earth where sinners are consigned and live for all eternity; good souls are resurrected, rising to heaven above. The Tower of Babel was an impious attempt to build a tower "whose top may reach heaven."

A few theologians and a majority of scientists rejected the flat-earth notion, preferring the spherical theory of Protagoras. As is well known, Columbus was convinced the earth was round and bravely sailed across Atlantic. His crew was less certain and believed they could be attacked by sea serpents waiting to devour ships, or that the horizon had an end and they would fall off the edge into perdition. The common belief was that the sun was red in the evening because it looked down on hell.

Our cosmic picture is quite different, of course: the Earth, an elliptical planet orbiting the sun. We no longer fear the thunderbolt as God's punishment, or treat comets as omens, cower at eclipses, or hesitate to use medicine for physical or mental illness. We have harnessed atmospheric electricity, and church steeples have lightning rods. We don't hesitate to circumnavigate the globe, orbit the world in space capsules, or land on the moon, and many of the solar planets may soon be pockmarked with human footprints.

Poets sometimes deplore the way that science has removed the romance of nature by analyzing the natural causes of everything, from falling stars to rainbows. The worry is that science murders to dissect. William Blake calls a star the "bright torch of love" and the "fair-haired angel of the evening," but physicists describe stars as emitting electro-magnetic radiation as a result of nuclear reactions. Goethe refers to the moon's "sweet soothing eye...watching like a gentle friend," and Shelley asks of the moon, "Art thou pale for weariness,/ Of climbing heaven and gazing on the earth...?" But astronomers speak of lunar volcanoes and impact craters, a structure formed from dust and gases, the crystallization of a magma ocean. Today we do not wonder how many angels can stand on the head of a pin but how much information can be stored on a microchip.

In the Middle Ages various astronomical events were given spiritual meaning, including comets, meteors, eclipses, and rainbows, the movement of the moon and stars, day and night, the waxing and waning of the sun in summer and winter. Churchmen saw these phenomena as signs, omens, and warnings, whereas scientists sought explanations in physical laws.

For example, comets were seen by religious leaders as divine signs, often foretelling the birth of a great man. A radiant sky is said to have surrounded the birth of Moses, the Chinese sage Lao-tze, and Gautama the Buddha, and a heavenly light led the Magi to the manger of Christ. Earlier, comets were viewed as fireballs or thunderbolts thrown by an angry god such as Zeus. The myth of dragons might have originated in fiery, long-tailed comets.

Comets also functioned as warning signs, which is how most Schoolmen interpreted them. "Comets portend revolutions of kingdoms, pestilence, war, winds, or heat," Origen wrote, and this view was endorsed by St Thomas Aquinas. A comet was believed to foretell the Norman conquest, literally woven into history by the Bayeux tapestry. In fact, comets as portents became an article of faith throughout Europe.

Queen Elizabeth I referred to comets, eclipses, and falls of snow as warnings against sin. She prescribed an "order of prayer to avert [His] wrath...to be used in all parish churches." At the same time, Martin Luther in Germany sermonized, "The heathen write that the comet may arise from natural causes, but God does not create one that does not foretoken a sure calamity."

Sometimes comets were called harlot stars, doing the work of the devil. The theologian, Andreas Celichius went so far as to identify comets as signs of human depravity, visible to mortals. The vapor is "the thick smoke of human sins, rising every day, every hour, every moment, full of stench and horror, before the face of God, and becoming gradually so thick as to form a comet." By contrast, some people today think "shooting stars" mean good luck.

The most notable example of comet superstition occurred during the Crusades. When Europeans armies were about to conquer Constantinople, a comet appeared, which alarmed the pope, Calixtus. He therefore decreed, "Several days of prayer... that whatever calamity impended might be turned from the Christians and against the Turks." Unfortunately, the prayers were not answered, even though Calixtus excommunicated the comet. The Moslems took Constantinople, which is Istanbul today. Halley's comet, as it came to be known, appears every 76 years.

From a scientific standpoint, comets are "celestial bodies composed of a solid mass at the center and a luminous tail of dust and gas. They have a cylindrical shape, a nucleus of 16x8x8 kilometers, and a tail of 20 million kilometers. Solar wind and interstellar dust blast their ions, dust and fragments, and their brilliant light is produced by the interaction of matter and antimatter."

We now understand that comets are composed of common elements of hydrogen, carbon, nitrogen, and oxygen, and that they circle the sun in an erratic, elliptical orbit. They are gigantic, dirty snowballs, and when the tail crosses in front of the sun, the crystals that compose them are illuminated. The Latin name *stella cometa* means literally "hairy star."

In the Middle Ages, meteor showers or falling stars were terrifying, and meant impending chaos, perhaps the end of the world. Alternatively, meteors appeared each time a baby was born; it was a candle lit in the sky. A falling star could indicate that a life has been extinguished.

Meteors that struck the earth were generally thought to come from heaven. This includes the black rock in the Kaaba at Mecca, worshipped as a holy object by Muslims. The legend is that it was once white but turned black because of human sin. Furthermore, in Islam, good angels are believed to throw showers of meteors at bad angels, driving them from the heavens.

From the perspective of astronomy, meteors are fallout from comets, and their collision with earth is predictable. We have 150 craters caused by meteors including Meteor Crater in Arizona and the Tunguska explosion, and the impact of a meteor caused the extinction of dinosaurs when a cloud of dust covered the sun.

Like comets, eclipses were always taken as emblematic of the gods' displeasure, foretelling imminent calamity. Darkness falling upon the earth during daylight hours was naturally taken as sign of disaster — a warning that God could withhold the light from the world forever. (This was the fear that preceded the winter solstice when each day was shorter and darker than the one before.) Eclipses occurred at the deaths of Prometheus, Hercules, Alexander the Great, Romulus, and Julius Caesar, which reinforced the view that they betokened evil. Charlemagne's son, Emperor Louis, may have died of fright at an eclipse, and as a result Europe was later divided into Germany, France, and Italy.

Eclipses were simply bad omens, a sign of catastrophe: if it was dark at midday, then the natural order was askew. The word 'eclipse' in Greek means abandonment, and people feared the light and warmth would desert them and never return. The sun gave life, and for it to be blotted out was a terrifying event. In Chinese mythology it was a great dragon that devoured the sun, and the people would pound on drums to frighten it away. In India the people immersed themselves in water to fight the sun-eating dragon.

Besides the darkness, eclipses had another fearful dimension. To the Medieval mind, they resembled the iris of the eye and could be viewed as God seeing every sin. A disk of blackness, with a white line around its edge is the eye of a God, glaring down from heaven in anger. The same interpretation was made of a lunar eclipse, especially since the moon is blood red as the shadow of the earth moves across it.

Numerous Biblical passages refer to eclipses: "And on that day I will make the Sun go down at noon, and darken the earth in broad daylight" (Amos); "The sun shall be turned into darkness and the moon into blood." (Acts); and "The sun will be darkened and the moon will not give its light" (Matthew). A solar eclipse allegedly occurred at the time of Christ's crucifixion ("There was darkness all over the land").

As we know, Columbus did not follow this religious view any more than he accepted a square world. When he landed in Jamaica the local people would not provide him with food and supplies. He knew from astrological charts that a lunar eclipse was due, so he threatened to make the moon disappear. When the moon began to fade, the terrified Jamaicans gave him everything he wanted. Once Columbus had his provisions, he made the moon return. This trick was also used by Mark Twain in *A Connecticut Yankee in King Arthur's Court.*

The scientific explanation, of course, is much simpler. Today we understand a solar eclipse as the obscuring of the sun's light by the intervention of the moon.

Contrary to eclipses, rainbows were usually taken as signs of a divine blessing and favor, a "charmed phenomenon." They were viewed as a tangible bridge of light leading to the divine. In *Genesis*, God displays a rainbow to seal a pact with humankind that he will not destroy the world again in a Flood. "I do set my bow in the cloud, and it shall be for a token of a covenant." (Partly as a religious exercise, schoolchildren in England were taught the rainbow's colors using the mnemonic, "Richard of York Gave Battle in Vain": red, orange, yellow, green, blue, indigo, and violet. Thanks to Newton we now realize that a spectrum of light appears when the sun shines through rain; the drops refract the light into variegated colors.

Science may diminish beauty by parting the veil of mystery surrounding such things as rainbows, but it can also enhance our appreciation of nature. Snow-capped mountains may be less majestic when geologists tell us about the temperature and pressure that formed them, but we are also able to admire them at another level, to wonder at the unimaginable forces that thrust them into the air. In the same way, when astronomers inform us that the sun is 93 million miles away from earth and its light takes 8 minutes to reach us, that can increase our sense of wonder. We certainly do not stop appreciating the sunrise or sunset. When we learn that the wind is tearing apart the molecules in clouds, we can still appreciate the billowy shapes that it forms. And we like the taste of apple pie even when we know how apples grow, and how pies are made.

Science also gives us power, and makes us feel less vulnerable. We need not fear natural phenomena quite so much once we understand the mechanisms driving them. We can even assume some measure of control, and feel more secure.

Of course, it does not cheer us up to learn that the universe will come to an end one day, Big Bang followed billions of years later by the Big Crunch, expansion then contraction to a subatomic dot. Or the end might come by the Big Rip, or the Heat Death, a bang or a whimper.

3. THE DECLINE OF RELIGION

Religious belief and observance are in decline throughout the Western world. Europe is largely secular, even though it is the home of cathedrals, sacred music, and devotional poetry. In the U.S., church attendance has declined precipitously, partly because of sex scandals in the Catholic Church, and the death of children in religious orphanages. Growing social acceptance of abortion and gay marriage has also contributed to the rift between the Church and society. And religion has encountered opposition due to freedom and individualism, more widespread education, and the identification between religion and war. Religion has often been used to justify war and to whip up the troops' enthusiasm.

But basically, a more fundamental change has occurred in how we view our place in the universe. That lies at the core of the retreat from religion.

Several polls, such as that of the Pew Research Center, indicate that only 19% to 26% of citizens in America attend church or synagogue today, slightly higher in the South and Midwest, lower in the Northeast. And if the present trend continues, in 20 years churchgoing will be 50% of what it is today. The culture is changing rapidly, and saying grace before meals or telling children to say their prayers before sleep seems archaic and outmoded.

A number of statistics and facts supporting the decline of religion in the U.S. are summarized in Ronald Inglehart's *Religion's Sudden Decline*. Here he writes that the United States has "showed the largest shift in any country *away* from religion and now ranks among the world's least religious publics." This is especially true since the 1990s.

The "nones" are a growing number, especially among the millennials, who tend to reject organized religion, and are less religious than their parents. They reject the formality, ritual, and ceremony of church services, and the average age of congregations is steadily increasing. But against all dire predictions, the young have not become wickeder. They seem conscientious about racism and sexism, helping the poor and disadvantaged, protecting animals and the environment — all without divine authority. Their values are not just personal preferences or community customs but a commitment to principles outside themselves. A secular ethic, independent of religion, seems possible.

Nationally, nonbelief is up from 16% in 2007 to 23% in 2000, or according to another statistic, 13% of Americans report that they are atheists. Since the 1990s, the number has been growing, and not attending church has become socially acceptable. Over the last 10 years, the country has moved from mostly believers to mostly nonbelievers. Religion may, in fact, be dying in the United States — and worldwide.

According to the *Huffington Post*, "For the first time in British [and Norwegian] history, there are now more atheists and agnostics than those who believe in God." "Nearly 76% of the Dutch are not affiliated with any religion, and according to a recent Eurobarometric Poll, 19% of Spaniards, 24% of Danes, 26% of Slovenians, 27% of Germans and Belgians, 34% of Swedes, and 40% of the French, claim not to believe in 'any sort of spirit, God, or life-force.'"

In Canada the number of nones has doubled since 1991, and in Australia, 15% had no religion in 2001; today the number stands at 22%. In New Zealand in 2001, 30% of the population claimed that they do not have any religion, but the number rose to 42% in 2013. The same trend has been recorded in Japan, S. Korea, China, and even in Africa.

On the planet in general, there were 11 billion non-religious people in 2010, which increased to over 12 billion by the year 2020.

Although the statistics are impressive, the number of atheists is probably under-reported. When people are asked whether they are religious, they tend to reply "Yes," because that is the respectable answer. But in fact, they may not believe in a supernatural being, attend church regularly, or have faith in life after death, with a system of rewards and punishments. Some will believe that death is simply the end, and some will believe we are punished by our sins not for them, and virtue is its own reward.

In any case, the trend seems clear, and it is hard to see what would reverse it. In America, we still incorporate religious terms and symbols in our civil ceremonies, but that may come to an end. In the Pledge of Allegiance, we have added the phrase "under God"; in court we swear to tell the truth "So help me God"; and presidents raise their right hand, and place their left hand on the Bible when they take the oath of office. In the future, when religion is not identified as an essential part of America, the separation of church and state might be enforced more vigorously.

There are a number of social, political, and economic reasons for the decline, especially having to do with the alignment of Republicans with traditional religion, and Democrats and Independents with nonreligion. (The conservative right has a much higher rate of affiliation, including evangelical religion.) However, the underlying reason seems to be a change in our worldview. The scientific explanation of the cosmos. its nature and structure, has won over the religious account. In every clash between the two, science has advanced and religion has retreated.

Most notably, Galileo's view of the earth revolving around the sun rather than the sun revolving around the earth has now been accepted as standard. It should have been accepted in 1632, but theologians refused to look through Galileo's telescope. They were afraid they would be convinced by fallible senses of something that they knew from the Bible to be false. Today we accept a heliocentric rather than a geocentric model, and it is a staple of contemporary astronomy. We also know that the Earth is a minor planet on the fringes of the Milky Way galaxy, and not the center of the universe. The planets and stars do not revolve around us.

And today we question whether each baby is a miraculous gift from God. Rather, we think that each human life was created by an ejaculation of 200 million sperm, that produced a single cell, that expanded to 39 trillion cells, kept alive by our heart beating 100,000 times each day. We know that all life is sustained by the sun, 93 million miles away, with cosmic objects measured in light years, the space covered by a ray of light traveling at 186,281 miles per second. And the sun is only one star among billions of stars in our galaxy, and there are billions of galaxies, a billion trillion stars.

And unlike the Biblical account, the universe has existed for 14 billion years, and human history lasts 10 seconds on the astronomical clock, the blink of an eye. Furthermore, the universe is expanding, carrying the earth with it, maybe expanding into nothing, or creating more of itself, infinite but curved. (It does seem curious that time come to an end at the edge of a black hole.)

Also, from the Middle Ages on, people had assumed the universe contains a plan, devised and set in motion by an intelligent God. It was assumed that every event, and human life itself, has a purpose. Nothing exists by accident or by chance. Everything happens for good reason, and serves a function in the grand scheme of things. This holds true from the largest to the smallest entity. The flea wakes the sluggard from his sleep, the mouse discourages untidiness in the kitchen. As Alfred Tennyson wrote,

> That not a moth with vain desire/ Is shrivell'd in a fruitless fire,... That not a worm is cloven in vain/ Or but subserves another's gain.

Human life is impoverished by the loss of this worldview, but we can't be willfully blind, and tell ourselves that we don't know what we do know. Wishful thinking can't be sustained for very long.

***

The argument for God's existence that is associated with design is called the Teleological Proof — 'telos' meaning end or reason. Briefly put, the argument states that when we look out at the world we are impressed with evidence of design. Rather than randomness and chaos, we see structure and order, an intentional plan, and the more science reveals of life the more impressive we are with the arrangement. The point is that if there is a design there must be a designer, just as the architecture of the universe implies a divine architect, and nature as a work of art, shows the brush strokes of God. In the same way, if there are natural laws, then there is a law-giver who enacted them. As Shakespeare wrote, there are "tongues in trees, books in the running brooks, sermons in stones."

In the 18th century, William Paley supported this argument in his *Natural Theology* with a famous Watchmaker Analogy. He argued that if we found a watch on the ground in perfect working order, we would be forced to conclude

> that the watch must have had a maker ... who formed it for the purpose which we find it actually to answer.
>
> In crossing a heath, suppose I pitched my foot upon a *stone*, and were asked how the stone came to be there, I might possibly answer, that for anything I knew to the contrary it had lain there forever; nor would it perhaps, be very easy to show the absurdity of this answer. But suppose I had found a *watch* upon the ground, and it should be inquired how the watch happened to be in that place, I should hardly think of the answer which I had before given, that for any thing I knew the watch might have always been there... Yet why should not this answer serve for the watch as well as for the stone; why is it not as admissible in the second case as in the first? For this reason, and for no other, namely that when we come to inspect the watch, we perceive — what we could not discover in the stone — that its several parts are framed and put together for a purpose, i.e., that they are so framed and adjusted as to produce motion, and that motion so regulated as to point out the hour of the day; that if the different parts had been differently shaped from what they are, or placed after any other manner or in any other order than that in which they are placed, either no motion at all would have been

carried on in the machine , or none which would have answered the use that is now served by it.

The inference we think is inevitable, that the watch must have had a maker — that there must have existed, at some time and at some place or other, an artificer or artificers who formed it for the purpose which we find it actually to answer, who comprehended its construction and designed its use. By analogy, when we encounter the intricate structure of the world, we must infer that it too had a maker; the parts could not have fallen together by chance in just the right combination to produce a perfectly functioning mechanism.

There cannot be a design without a designer," Paley wrote, "contrivance without a contriver; order without choice; arrangement without anything capable of arranging." That is, unless we assume "the presence of intelligence and mind" the world in its orderliness is inexplicable.

As a later theologian remarked "Everywhere we turn there are evidences of the unity of counsel and design," and even Voltaire conceded, "I cannot imagine how the clockwork of the universe exists without a clockmaker." Only God is sufficient to have produced the intricate structure of the earth, and everything that it contains.

Since the 18th century the Teleological Argument has been reinforced by various findings, for example, that the earth is perfectly positioned in the solar system to sustain life. If it were closer to the sun we would sizzle, farther away we would freeze to death — a kind of Goldilocks phenomenon. An ozone layer shields us from ultraviolet light, and a magnetic field protects us from radiation and high energy particles. And if the earth were too large a rock it would collapse into itself; too small it would spin off into space. In addition, an envelope of moisture surrounds the earth allowing just the right amount of precipitation, just as we have the ideal combination of gases for plants and animals to exist — oxygen, nitrogen, and oxygen. If the water on earth were too hot, it would vaporize; too cold, it would freeze into ice. Furthermore, human beings need to eat plants and animals, and edible plants and animals are provided. The marvelous mechanism of the human body itself points to a supreme designer who organized our complex systems and organs, our balanced chemistry and physiology for ideal functioning. The intricacy of the human eye and brain alone testify to the genius of creation. The world is simply too organized and beautiful to have been created naturally.

Evidence of design has also been cited within the animal kingdom where the attributes needed by different species have been perfectly distributed: the hard shell of the turtle, the ability of the chameleon to change color, and the giraffe's long neck enabling it to reach the leaves at the tops of trees. Birds have been given wings, the rhinoceros a thick hide, cheetahs speed, zebras camouflage, ducks waxed feathers, porcupines, quills, lions sharp teeth and claws, and so forth.

In his *Antidote Against Atheism*, the 17th century philosopher Henry More put it this way:

> For why have we three joints in our legs and arms, as also in our fingers, but that it was much better than having but two or four? And why are our fore-teeth broad to grind but that it is more exquisite than having them all sharp or all broad...Again, why are the teeth so luckily placed, or rather why are there not teeth in other bones as well as in the jawbone for they might have been as capable as these? But the reason is, Nothing is done foolishly or in vain; that is, there is a divine Providence that orders all things.

This is a strong case, and one that appeals to our common sense. Currently, it is sometimes called the argument from Intelligent Design, and emphasizes the complexity of the universe. Everything is too intricate to have come about by chance. It would be like blowing up a junk yard and having everything settle into place to form a 747, or a super computer.

Even those who reject the reasoning have paid tribute to its force. One philosopher Immanuel Kant wrote "This proof always deserves to be mentioned with respect. It is the oldest, the clearest and the most accordant with the common reason of mankind. It enlivens the study of nature...[and] so strengthens the belief in a supreme Author of nature that the belief acquires the force of an irresistible conviction." Another philosopher, David Hume, wrote, "A purpose, an intention, a design strikes everywhere the most careless, the most stupid thinker, and no man can be so hardened in absurd systems as at all times to reject it... all the sciences almost lead us insensibly to acknowledge a first Author."

However, even though the argument is a traditional one, and it does seem self-evident that "design implies a designer," there are problems with it. The most obvious defect is that the world is not the kind we would expect from a loving God, who is perfect and wholly good. Being omniscient and omnipotent, he had all options at his disposal, and the ability to create a different scenario than he did, but there is chaos as well as order, entropy as well as development. More important, there are conditions on earth that cause suffering to human beings. Natural catastrophes and disasters, accidents, sickness, and disease seem built into the design — from floods to earthquakes to avalanches, from cholera to malaria to leukemia. And there are savage animals on earth, inhospitable environments, killing cold and burning heat. The habitat created for man is not consistently kind but filled with swamps, deserts, mountains, jungles, and oceans. Why make the earth one third water, and not give people gills?

Furthermore, the pain experienced by animals is substantial, and would be reduced if all creatures were herbivores. Why should there be carnivorous creatures that slaughter each other for food? Why create a system of predators and prey? Furthermore, the marvelous mechanism of the human body breaks down regularly, or we would not have such an enormous medical establishment. And why give man life, then take back a third of it in sleep?

We wonder, therefore, about the benevolence of the plan — or even whether any plan exists. The assumption that human suffering is random not intentional might be more plausible. This is behind the remark of the writer Jules Renard: "I don't know if God exists, but it would be better for his reputation if he didn't."

However, the main problem facing the Teleological Argument is an alternative theory offered by the 19th century biologist Charles Darwin in a book that changed the world: *The Origin of Species*. Here Darwin offered as a substitute a natural explanation for the orderliness that exists. He claimed that if turtles had not possessed hard shells, chameleons the ability to change color, or giraffes, long necks, and so forth they would not have survived as a species. These were the mutations called for in the life struggle, so it is not remarkable that species now living possess the characteristics they need to survive. To think that it's uncanny would be like being surprised that all Olympic winners are good athletes; if they were not good athletes, they would not be Olympic winners. Or it would be like being amazed that so many major cities are situated beside navigable rivers; if the rivers had not been navigable, they would not have become major cities.

Similarly, we can understand the ideal position of the earth relative to the sun, the edibleness of plants and animals, and the efficient functioning of the human body. If these factors had not been the case, we would not have the world we do. All aspects of life have evolved in accordance with the principle of natural selection and survival of the fittest.

According to the anthropological evidence, we once lived in trees, then climbed down onto the savannah; we once walked on four legs, then on two. At one time we had scaly fins, then hairy paws, and now a skin-covered hand. Our limbs were protrusions from protoplasm for locomotion and grasping. Our eye was a light-sensitive cell

In a famous debate Bishop Wilberforce asked the biologist Thomas Huxley (Darwin's bulldog) whether it was from his grandmother or his grandfather that he claimed descent from monkeys. Huxley replied that he would not be ashamed of ape ancestors but only of arrogance and closed-mindedness. Evolutionists see a common ancestry for both human beings and the higher apes.

Also, Sir John Lightfoot claimed that the universe began at exactly 9:00 A.M., on October 23rd, 3927 B.C., but Darwin maintained there had been an evolution over millions of years. Contemporary scientists have confirmed this through radiocarbon dating of rocks, fossils, and the earth itself. Astronomers now estimate the start of the universe with the explosion of Big Bang occurring about 13.7 billion years ago, the sun as forming 9 billion years later, the earth as 4.5 billion years old, and the genus *Homo* as having existed for several million years; the oldest skeleton discovered to date, a female known to science as Ardi, which is placed at 4.4 million years. *Homo sapiens* (or homo but not very sapien) originated some 200,000 years ago. And all species were not made through instantaneous creation at a fixed point in time, but new species developed over millions of years as evidenced by fossil remains; chimpanzees or bonobos are our closest relative.

In essence, Darwin offered a naturalistic explanation in place of a supernatural one, and that view is accepted today by scientists and the general public. If we hear hoof beats, we should think horse before we think zebra.

Although God might lie behind evolution, using it as his instrument, adding God may not be necessary. As "Occam's razor" states, we should not compound explanations beyond what is required; the simplest theory is best. Since evolution can explain the order of the world in natural, comprehensive terms, it is superfluous to add a God as being behind it. When the mathematician de Laplace presented his treatise on celestial mechanics to Napoleon, the emperor remarked, "I see no mention of God here." Laplace replied, "I had no need of that hypothesis." In the same way, according to Occam's Razor, adding God is unnecessary to explain the world.

How could life have come about without God? The scientific answer is that DNA was produced by nucleotides when successful molecules replicated themselves. Water and amino acids, which are necessary for life, were contained in comets and asteroids that bombarded the earth 4 billion years ago.

Furthermore, the evolutionists argue that it is difficult to account for the extinction of dinosaurs using the biblical account of creation but it can be explained in terms of the Darwinian model. After ruling for one hundred sixty million years, dinosaurs could not survive an asteroid strike. The impact threw up a cloud of dust, blocking the sun, chilling the earth, and killing most plants the dinosaurs needed for food. In fact, over time, hundreds of thousands of species became extinct when they could not adapt to changing conditions, and only fossils remain to show that they once existed. As some philosophers have pointed out, it would be odd for God to recall dinosaurs and to try mammals instead, that is, to change his mind.

In defense of the religious view, theologians sometimes used questionable arguments such as "Our ancestors might have been apes, but God adopted us," or "God planted fossils on earth to test our faith," or "He created the earth with these imprints." But the Darwinists reply that, yes, *for all we know* God made the earth complete with fossils, just as oysters might be doing differential equations, and hibernating bears might be dreaming of the periodic table of the elements. But *as far as we know* they are not. Similarly, it seems more reasonable to regard fossils as preserved remains of living organisms, some of which are now extinct. Geologists debate whether fossils are bone or stone, but no one doubts they existed well before 4000 B.C. As for marine fossils on the tops of mountains, including Mt. Everest, that does not prove the Flood but rather the upheavals of ice ages when levels of earth changed and sea levels rose.

Furthermore, theology plays a dangerous game if it calls 'God' whatever we do not know. For then the more we know, the less room there is for God. In this way, religion is edged out of the universe. That has, in fact, been the pattern. No one knew what caused lightning, locusts, earthquakes, or plagues so these events were ascribed to the power of God, but that meant that the more science explained, the less was attributed to God. Historically, as science uncovered causes that were unknown, religion has declined in power, maybe edged out as a primitive account. The divine cannot be used as an explanation for what we do not know. A "God of the gaps" is vulnerable.

***

One popular argument has recently been resurrected from Blaise Pascal, a 17th Century mathematician and philosopher, who proposed a practical proof of God. In "Pascal's Wager" he argued that if we believe there is a God, and we're right, we go straight to heaven when we die; and if we're wrong, we still have a pleasant life on earth; we then feel there is divine protection, support for our values, and an ultimate meaning to life. On the other hand, if we don't believe in God, and we're wrong, we go to hell when we die, and our life on earth is drained of significance. The choice is obvious: we should believe in God, because right or wrong, we are better off.

This reasoning seems persuasive; however it may be too self-serving. Pascal urges us to believe in God for our sake not for his sake, and God, as depicted in Western religion, would reject belief based on selfish reasons. What's more, Pascal's Wager is not an argument for the existence of God, but for believing in the existence of God. As stated earlier, we cannot get our minds round to accepting an idea because it would do us good, but only because we are convinced it is true.

The argument has also been criticized because we should then accept any number of beliefs just to hedge our bets and be on the safe side. If it were beneficial, we would accept the Hindu deities and a Muslim heaven, astrology, witchcraft, and magic — just in case. We would be able to argue that if we're right we have everything to gain, and if we are wrong, we lose nothing, so why not accept every possible belief. A position of that nature does not seem sound or even useful.

Aside from arguments, the sentiments of the "nones" are in keeping with the temper of the times. Atheism has permeated the modern consciousness, and a secular worldview is increasingly common. Yuri Gagarin, the first man in space, said he did not see God anywhere. People today are less likely to turn to a minister, priest or rabbi for advice, but to friends or family, a support network for help. We rely on the services of doctors, lawyers, therapists, accountants, teachers, technicians, and so on rather than the confessional or religious counseling. In the Middle Ages people naturally turned to God for help, and they lived their lives against a backdrop of divine purpose. They wondered what they were meant to do with their lives, where they fit in God's plan. But today we feel alone, and must work out the terms of our existence for ourselves, removed from spiritual guidance.

Like Dostoevsky some say, "If God is dead, then everything is permissible," but that does not tell us what life to pursue or how to conduct ourselves. And rather than feeling liberated, we are left with a sense of confusion, disorientation, and loss.

In *The Joyful Wisdom*, by the 19th-century German philosopher Friedrich Nietzsche, this feeling of absence and abandonment is poignantly expressed. A "madman" screams to a crowd,

> Whither is God? We *have killed him* — you and I. All of us are his murderers. But how have we done this? How were we able to drink up the sea? Who gave us the sponge to wipe away the entire horizon? What did we do when we unchained this earth from its sun? Whither is it moving now? Whither are we moving now? Away from all suns? Are we not straying as through an infinite nothing? Do we not feel the breath of empty space?... God is dead. God remains dead. And we have killed him. How shall we, the murderers of all murderers, comfort ourselves? What was holiest and most powerful of all that the world has yet owned has bled to death under our knives.... Is not the greatness of this deed too great for us? Must not we ourselves become gods simply to seem worthy of it?"

To Nietzsche, "God is dead" in the sense that people no longer believe in him. He is dead to people in the modern world, and that is cause for eulogies and grief. It seems inconceivable that man can kill God, extinguish the sun, and now we must become gods ourselves, and find our way alone.

One interesting question is, "If religion is fiction, but reassures and comforts us, should we try to abolish it?" What should be done with the beneficial myth? Should we discard it because it is a myth, or retain it because it is beneficial?

The problem is that once we reject God, then that idea no longer offers comfort and we can't believe in him for the consolation it provides. Pragmatism tells us we should accept religion because it works for us, but we can only believe in something if we know it is true. Then the benefits or detriments will follow. But we can't bring our minds round to accepting an idea because it's good for us to think so. That way lies self-deception, which cannot be sustained for very long. We have too much self-respect to convince ourselves that we do know what we don't know — however positive that might be for our mental health.

4. THE PLACE OF VALUES IN A WORLD OF FACT

Because we live in a physical/material world, people are perplexed about moral decisions. Is anything really right or wrong, and how do we judge?

We used to think of God as validating our social norms. The Ten Commandments and The Sermon on the Mount provided the foundation for our conduct. We knew that we should not kill or lie, steal or commit adultery because the Bible said so, and the Bible was the word of God. Scripture was the inspired word of the Lord; he was moving the pen, or speaking into the ear of scribes.

But as God has receded from our consciousness, and divine authority has diminished, we wonder whether there are any rules at all, or just an amoral world, a trackless wasteland. And even if we regard the Bible as a holy, infallible book, the pronouncements are far too general to be of much help, as well as being ambiguous and contradictory. Differences between the Old Testament and the New Testament raise one type of problem; but even within the New Testament there are mutually contradictory passages, different versions of the same story, and puzzling scenarios that leave us unsure of the moral message. Should we kill in war if our cause is just ("just" according to whose perspective?), and lie if it would result in the greater good? Can we steal, if a person acquired his wealth unfairly and was oppressing the society, and would it be adultery if we lusted after another person but never acted on it? We don't know which values are of overriding importance, taking precedence over others.

In the New Testament varying genealogies are given for Jesus — that his father was Joseph, or Jacob, or Heli, all of which are at variance with Mary's immaculate conception by the Holy Spirit. Matthew (51:2) states Jesus gave his sermon on the mountain; in Luke (6:17–20) it was on the plain. According to John (19:17), Jesus carried his own cross, but Mark (15:21–23) says Simon carried the cross. Matthew and Mark report that the last words of Jesus were "My God, my God, why hast thou forsaken me?" but Luke says they were "Father, into thy hands I commend my spirit."

Rather than scripture being inerrant, it seems more reasonable to assume it is the product of early peoples trying to make sense of their world in a simplistic way. Furthermore, their stories were written down years, even centuries, after the events they reported, and stories that are passed on by word of mouth will invariably change from person to person. Even if the Bible is infallible, people do not interpret it infallibly, so the Bible must contain some mistakes; to err is human.

Be that as it may, even if we retain belief in God, and revere scripture, that would not provide a basis for values. Contrary to popular belief, the only connection between religion and ethics is psychological, not logical.

The distinction between the two goes back to ancient Greece, specifically to a Platonic dialogue called *The Euthyphro*. Here, Socrates meets a man named Euthyphro on the porch of a Court called the King Archon. Socrates is there to defend himself against an accusation of impiety. He has been charged by two Athenian citizens, Meletus and Anytus, of corrupting the youth with sacrilegious teachings. Euthyphro is there to prosecute his father for murder. Apparently, his father had punished a slave boy for some offense by tying him up and throwing him into a ditch. The boy died of exposure overnight, and Euthyphro thinks this is a sin against the gods, an impiety. He believes his father deserves to be punished for sacrilege.

Socrates professes to feel fortunate at having met Euthyphro, because anyone confident enough to charge his own father with a crime must know a great deal about piety and what is right and wrong. That knowledge could help Socrates in his own defense. So, he asks Euthyphro to define piety. Euthyphro first answers that it is what he is doing at the moment: bringing even his father to justice if there has been a wrongdoing. But Socrates rejects this definition, saying that he doesn't want an example or illustration of piety but needs to understand its nature. It would be like defining music by saying that some people play the harp or flute, others the drums.

Euthyphro then proposes that piety is what is beloved of the gods, and the impious is what they hate. After some byplay about the Olympian gods sometimes disagreeing amongst themselves, Socrates poses a key question: Is an action pious because the gods love it, or do they love it because it is pious?

These alternatives may seem the same, but there's a crucial difference. If an action is right because the gods love it, then ethics is based on religion. But if an action is loved by the gods because it is right, then ethics is independent of religion because actions are right in themselves.

Socrates forces Euthyphro to the conclusion that actions are intrinsically right (or wrong) and are loved (or not) for that reason. Otherwise, the gods could make the right wrong and the wrong right if they so chose, making kindness wrong and cruelty right. They would judge actions in an arbitrary way, maybe by their personal disposition, or on a whim. But if the gods have good reason for approving actions, then it is because they recognize their inherent rightness, that which makes them worthy of being loved.

The dialogue aims to show that ethics does not come from religion but stands apart from it. In terms of our current monotheism, actions are not right because God loves them, but God loves them because they are right. Saints and sinners are identified as such by God, not made so by decree. This means that the death of God need not have any impact on ethical values, because they never came from God to begin with. He only recognized their moral nature and commanded them because he found them right.

Psychologically, we associate ethics with religion and feel that in the absence of God, ethics has no foundation. But *The*

Euthyphro shows us that, logically, religion cannot be the basis for ethics, and the loss of God does not entail the absence of right and wrong. People can continue to be judged praiseworthy or blameworthy, because God was irrelevant to moral value at the outset.

***

A way forward is indicated by the Universal Declaration of Human Rights, a document that is respected world-wide even in our factual age. It was passed unanimously by the General Assembly of the United Nations and specifies the minimum standards that nations should uphold for their citizens. The atrocities of World War II showed that a document of this kind was needed, a set of universal standards applicable to all countries. Eleanor Roosevelt, who chaired the U.N. Commission on Human Rights, drafted the Declaration along with several others, and she called it humanity's Magna Carta.

In the Preamble it states,

> Whereas recognition of the inherent dignity and of the equal and inalienable right of all members of the human family is the foundation of freedom, justice and peace in the world, Whereas disregard and contempt for human rights has resulted in barbarous acts which have outraged the conscience of mankind, Whereas the advent of a world in which human beings shall enjoy freedom of speech and belief, and freedom from fear and want has been proclaimed as the highest aspiration of the common people, Whereas it is essential if man is not to be compelled to have recourse, as a last resort, to rebellion against tyranny and oppression, that human rights should be protected by the rule of law... the peoples of the United Nations have in the Charter reaffirmed their faith in fundamental human rights, in the dignity and worth of the human person and in the equal rights of men and women...Therefore THE GENERAL ASSEMBLY proclaims this UNIVERSAL DECLARATION OF HUMAN RIGHTS as a common standard of achievement for all peoples and all nations.

There follow thirty articles that cover the fundamental rights and freedoms of people throughout the world. Included among these are the right to life, liberty, and security of person; to freedom from arbitrary arrest, to a fair trial; to be presumed innocent until proved guilty; to freedom from interference with the privacy of one's home and correspondence; to freedom of movement and residence; to asylum, nationality, and ownership of property; to freedom of thought, conscience, religion, opinion, and expression; to association, peaceful assembly, and participation in government; to social security, work, rest, and a standard of living adequate to health and well-being; to education, and to participation in the social life of one's community.

The Declaration of Human Rights was passed, although several of the communist nations abstained. They regarded it as an assault on their national sovereignty, an intrusion on their internal affairs. Some criticized it as neo-imperialist. Nevertheless, the Declaration is considered a fundamental baseline of human well-being. The signatories thought of these rights as inalienable and universal.

It is hard to argue against these rights. They are not valuable because people value them, but people value them because they are right. Ethics does not depend on majority rule, or popularity, but on human good. To say that values are relative to a society, and that we should be tolerant of all values, is self-defeating, because in declaring tolerance the ultimate good, a universal judgment is being made.

***

It is possible to make sense of our world in terms of shared human experience, without a higher source of values. Religion is not necessary for reference, although it does provide urgency to moral behavior. (Sometimes it motivates people to immoral behavior, as in the case of the Taliban.) By participating in science and reason, society and politics, culture, and the arts, we can we can become aware of what fulfills us, be responsive to human suffering, and feel a responsibility to improve other's lives. We can realize our interests and needs outside the framework of religion, and understand which of our desires are enhancing and which are destructive. Some of our desires, of course, are in-between and hard to classify, but the fact of twilight does not mean it is impossible to differentiate between night and day. Our ethics should not be built on the outliers.

We now understand that human beings are intelligent animals, who have evolved from simpler forms of life. We are the end-product that began as specks of protoplasmic jelly in the scum of tides that then crawled out of the primordial ooze. We have evolved through chance mutations from fish to amphibians to animals, culminating in the human species. Brute matter has become self-conscious in man, who can try to understand where he fits in the scheme of things, and find values and purpose in living. We have developed to the point where we don't just react but act, making conscious choices, and we restrain our worst impulses through what is called conscience.

Human beings seem to be free and creative beings, curious and inventive, and those virtues should be allowed to flourish. Contrary to Behaviorism, people have an inner world of emotions and feelings that should be expressed.

Religion sometimes interferes with human needs, conceiving of a supreme being who rules the universe with a preordained plan, and who knows our every thought and action. He rewards those who obey him with heaven, and assigns those who doubt his word to the fires of hell. Free thought is judged to be sacrilegious. When disasters happen, the religious assume it is their fault. They search their soul for the sins that caused a catastrophe to fall on their heads, and try to placate the wrath of God so it does not happen again. In the past, leaders have referred droughts, famines, or military defeats to God's retribution for the people's wrongdoing, thereby escaping personal blame. Rulers have set themselves up as God's representative on earth, the voice of the Lord, and declared that their governance could not be questioned. The fault lay with people's sinfulness.

Some liberal religion often share the values articulated in the Universal Declaration of Human Rights, and they deserve to be followed, not because they come from religion, but because they appear right. The baby does not have to be thrown out with the bath water (or holy water); the ethics can be accepted without the metaphysics. We do not need to believe in a supernatural authority, a divine spark in our soul, in order for values to be authentic or living to be worthwhile. Life can have meaning even if the soul is only the "I," and nothing of ourselves survives after death. A human-oriented, value system can be trusted, without a supernatural source to certify it. Human dignity and worth seem valuable in and of themselves.

The emphasis should be on satisfying human needs, and solving human problems through good will and understanding. There is no "forbidden knowledge" nothing that we should not know, but we must be vigilant about new discoveries, and exercise moral restraint upon them so they contribute too human good. In the absence of divine guidance, we have to take responsibility for our own lives, and those of our fellow man.

Within ourselves we have the potential to be kind and just, to improve our character and make the world more humane. History has shown that we also have the capacity for cruelty and violence, but these tendencies are more than balanced by our impulses toward generosity and compassion. This is the only life we will have, so we should actualize our latent abilities, become fully ourselves, within the confines of the welfare of others.

We cannot actualize every aspect of ourselves; we haven't the time, and one facet of our being would inevitably conflict with another. Rather, we have to develop under the guidance of our dominant interests. This provides a principle of selection when we wonder which action we should choose. We ought to develop as broadly as possible, in keeping with our essential self. That is more important than the variety or diverse range of our development.

The American philosopher George Santayana explains the point this way: "It is characteristic of the absolute romantic spirit that when it is finished with something it must invent a new interest. It beats the bushes for fresh game; it is always on the verge of being utterly bored.... [However] man is constituted by his limitations, by his station contrasted with all other stations, and by his purpose chosen from amongst all other purposes. His understanding may render him universal; his life never can. To be at all, you must be something in particular." If we are everything in general, we are nothing in particular; we have no identity, and are like a set of random numbers. To become an individual, we must decide who we want to become.

In choosing to develop our qualities we must imagine our ideal self, the person who would exist if we maximized our interests, talents, and abilities. Of course, we are never complete. We always fall short of our goal because the horizon line moves as we do, but in the process, we thrive and grow. And the ideal of full development gives direction to our lives. In the same way, mankind will never attain perfection, but it encourages us to have a goal, to know that there are values to pursue — without religion and even in a world of fact.

5. Intention, Consequence, and the Worth of an Action

Today we tell ourselves it's the result that counts; that the way to hell is paved with good intentions. What matters is the effect, the consequence or outcome of an action. Was the result beneficial or harmful? If the act did some good, then it can be praised; if it caused harm, then it has to be condemned, and the fact that the person meant well is irrelevant.

Whatever happens is observable; it is extant, and can be judged. But what the person had in mind is forever unknowable. Maybe the person didn't realize the gun was loaded, but that does not affect the fact that he shot someone. Whether he should have checked the gun beforehand can affect the severity of the offense — say, manslaughter or murder, in various degrees, but the person is still responsible for someone's death. Even the soldier who mistakenly shoots a civilian in "the fog of war" is still held accountable. An honest mistake is still a mistake, and the fact that the soldier did not mean to do it does not set things right. It was not an accident because accidents happen, but people are the ones who make mistakes.

If you try hard but come in second, you still finished in second place. Maybe it was your personal best, but you lost, and that is what matters in the end. When we receive a bad present, we console ourselves by saying, it's the thought that counts.

But it's still a bad present. As Chairman Mao said, in justifying capitalist features in the communist state, "It doesn't matter whether the cat is black or white, as long as it catches mice." The ultimate test is not whether the ideology is correct, but whether it brings about the social good.

We usually regard a good decision as one that works out well, although some argue that a good decision is one based on sound reasons; the vagaries of fortune determine the outcome. But on the consequentialist view, good decisions are the first, those that succeed, not fail. If the investment yields a high return, it was a good investment; if the medicine cures the illness, it's an efficacious medicine; if the horse you bet on comes in first, it was a good bet. The proof of the pudding is always in the eating, not the cooking.

An alternative view to consequentialism is that of intentionalism. Here the intention, motive, or purpose of the agent behind the action is what matters most. Why something is done is more important than what is done, or its aftereffects.

Robin Hood is a folk hero because, according to legend, he stole from the rich to give to the poor. He was a thief, but his motive was pure. He did not steal to become wealthy, but to improve the lives of the destitute and hungry. And we can forgive the "robber barons," in part, because after making a fortune through monopolies in railroads, steel, petroleum, and gold, they established philanthropic institutions such as the Rockefeller Foundation, Vanderbilt University, and Carnegie Hall. In their business practices they were unscrupulous, even ruthless, but their later generosity made up for some of the harm they did — and it was not all public relations. Being charitable did improve their public image, but it might still be altruistically motivated.

Conversely, an insurance company that distributes information on health and safety probably wants to reduce claims; their intention is to improve growth and profit, the bottom line, not the welfare of humanity. A beverage company that switches to plastic bottles probably is not doing so to prevent injuries caused by broken glass bottles, but packaging their product more cheaply. A sign saying "Turn out the lights when not in use," is probably designed to save money on electricity, not to save the planet. If you believe in keeping your friends close and your enemies closer, that is not because you love your enemies. And when a company says it's here to serve you, that is disingenuous: their product is a means of obtaining profit for themselves. Helping others is a by-product of their primary, self-serving purpose.

On this view, if we do the right thing for the wrong reasons, that negates the worth of the action. Or as William Blake famously said in *Auguries of Innocence*, "A truth that's told with bad intent beats all the lies you can invent." Whether someone jumped or was thrown off a roof makes a difference, even though it comes to the same thing in the end.

In law *mens rea*, or an evil mind, is an important concept. If a murder is committed "with malice aforethought," that is much worse than accidental, vehicular homicide, or even felony murder. Anyone who commits premeditated murder, such as the Mafia "hit man," is given the maximum sentence, whereas someone who kills by mistake is punished lightly, if at all.

Killing in self-defense is excusable because the person did not mean to kill but only to save their own life; they killed not out of malice but for self-preservation. For the same reason, a witness on the stand may plead the Fifth Amendment against self-incrimination, because the law cannot compel people to harm themselves, any more than a person is expected to allow their lives to be taken rather than protect themselves, and even kill if necessary.

And we can tell what a person meant to do, distinguishing between first degree murder and manslaughter, as was mentioned. If someone had planned the crime, has a motive for killing, buys a weapon to carry out his plan, was seen in the vicinity, and brags about his actions to some friends, that constitutes good evidence that the murder was premeditated. If, on the other hand, someone knocks over a flower pot on the ledge of a building and it kills someone walking below, that seems unintentional, especially if there's no connection between the perpetrator and the victim.

The intentionalist also claims that our reason for doing something is always within our control, but the same cannot be said for the results of our actions. This is why Christianity maintains that coveting your neighbor's wife is the same as committing adultery. The assumption is that lust is within our power. In fact, the thought may be even more sinful than the deed, because it allows the devil inside of us. You've committed adultery in your heart, and are not being ruled by God.

Some critics disagree with this assessment because our desires may not be under our control. The foods we like, our taste in art, our attraction to someone, may not be a matter of will, or be capable of changing. People can't be persuaded to feel differently about liking anchovies, or a painting by Picasso, and sometimes trying to persuade someone otherwise is counterproductive. The hell-fire-and-brimstone preacher who tells his congregation, "You must avoid lust, remember, lust is a sin, lust, lust, is evil," leaves his congregation thinking only about lust. It is similar to a mean game that can be played with children. You can tell a child there's a treasure hidden in the garden, but they can only find it if they don't think of a white rabbit. When the children look for it, all they can think of is a white rabbit, and, of course, they return empty handed. They must keep in mind what they have to put out of their mind, to remember what they need to forget. This is a double-bind, a psychological conflict.

Judging actions by their consequences is the hard-nosed view, and relates to our respect for visible, tangible phenomena. Having your heart in the right place matters, but not as much as positive, tangible results.

Of course, judging by results can be depersonalizing and numbing. As Stalin said, "The death of one man is tragic, but the death of thousands is a statistic." The number of young men killed in battle does not seem to discourage a nation from going to war again, and killing people in a bombing raid at 30,000 feet does not bring home the horrors of war the way killing a man in hand-to-hand combat does.

However, besides consequences or intentions, another way of judging actions steers a course between those alternatives. We can judge actions according to their moral nature, that is, their inherent rightness or wrongness. Some actions seem right in terms of human welfare, others are wrong in that they are destructive to mankind, and both intention and consequence are irrelevant.

This is a formalist position, and it trades on our respect for values and principles. Some formalists assert that an action is right if it enhances human life, for example, truth-telling and promise-keeping. We have an obligation to tell the truth, and to keep our word. In the same way, we have a responsibility to preserve life not take life, to be kind rather than cruel, to protect children and not take advantage of their weakness to exploit them. Honesty is more valuable than deceit, being nourished is better than going hungry, being safe and sheltered superior to being exposed and living in danger. We should choose health over sickness, friendship over enmity, peace over war, justice instead of discrimination, be fair not biased, generous not selfish, give people what they deserve, and so forth.

There is a standard of conduct that the world's peoples accept, a set of principles that are not right because people agree to them, but people agree to them because they are seen as right. Certain values are respected, and guide human relationships in our daily interactions. Even children know they should share, and that the game is unfair if someone doesn't wait his turn. While allowing for cultural differences, it seems basic that love is better than hate, life is better than death. We affirm the value of life by living it, and not choosing to end it.

These virtues seem banal because their rightness is self-evident, which does not mean evident to oneself, but apparent to anyone who is being honest. And people should be judged by whether they adhere to such standards, or violate them for their personal advantage.

***

Law and ethics do allow for excusing conditions, by which people are exempt from blame (or praise) for their actions. For instance, people are not responsible if they are acting from compulsion. If someone's finger is forced over the trigger of a gun, the person cannot be held accountable if the gun fires, and someone is hurt. The person could not do otherwise, and that is a complete excuse. If a car has a steering failure, and a pedestrian is struck, the driver could not help it. Provided the car had regular maintenance, and the steering had been checked by a competent technician, the driver could not anticipate the failure. If a sentry is drugged, he shouldn't be brought up on charges of dereliction of duty when he was unable to carry out his mission. A train engineer who has an epileptic seizure, and did not know he was an epileptic, bears no responsibility if the train crashes. He could not control the train, and so cannot be blamed.

In psychological terms, if someone is psychotic, and hears voices (that he must obey), telling him to set fire to a building, he should not be charged with arson. His mental illness precluded him from acting otherwise. The serial killer, "Son of Sam," claimed a demon manifested in a dog told him to kill people, and he did what he was told. Those with Obsessive Compulsive Disorder (OCD), can feel driven to hoarding. eating, gambling, talking, shopping, video games, or stealing, even if the activity is irrational or pointless. People can be mentally incompetent to stand trial.

In addition to compulsion, physical or psychological, people are not responsible for their actions if they are done in ignorance — unavoidable ignorance. A doctor cannot excuse himself from blame by saying he didn't know the latest treatment for a disease. As a physician, he has a responsibility to keep himself informed by reading the medical journals. Or if a bridge collapses, the civil engineer who designed it cannot claim as an excuse that he did not know the steel would not bear the weight of cars. Part of engineering is knowing the strength of materials. However, if a company markets talcum powder for babies, and does not know it is carcinogenic, the company is not responsible for the harm that resulted. According to the state-of-the-art at the time, it was considered harmless, and no one knew otherwise. And if a tree falls on a car, injuring the occupants, the driver cannot blame himself for the harm that occurred, because he could not have anticipated that the tree would fall. He did not know, and could not know.

Sometimes we blame ourselves for things that happen, thinking that if it weren't for us, the event would not have occurred. But a necessary condition, without which something wouldn't happen, is not the same as the cause of it happening. Having life is needed for death; if we never lived, we would not die, but life does not cause death. In the above example, if the driver did not make the trip, the tree would not have fallen on the car, but he did not cause the tree to fall and could not have foreseen that it would. It was a tragic accident, wholly beyond his control.

In Sophocles' *Oedipus Rex*, Oedipus kills his father and marries his mother, but he does so inadvertently, not consciously or willingly. He was a plaything of the gods, and everything that happened was destined to occur. Oedipus could not know that Laius, the man he killed, was his father, his wife Jocasta, was his mother, and even though patricide and incest were the limit of horror to the Greek mind, he was not to blame. Jocasta hangs herself in shame, and Oedipus puts out his eyes; there are some things we cannot bear to see. But Oedipus was cursed. He could not avoid his fate, and should not have punished himself with blindness. "O heavy hand of fate!!/ Who now more desolate, / Whose tale more sad than thine."

In court, the insanity defense trades on both compulsion and ignorance. A defendant is acquitted of a crime if a mental disorder forced him to act, or he lacked "substantial capacity to appreciate the wrongfulness of the conduct, or to conform to the requirements of law." We no longer believe in demonic possession, and "the devil made me do it" is not a viable excuse, but we do allow a plea of not guilty by reason of insanity.

***

But if people are considered responsible for their actions, then we must decide whether the intention, the consequence, or the nature of the act is the most important factor.

Intention is sometimes dismissed because the person behind the action is being judged rather than the action itself. We are evaluating the individual's character. The consequences of action are criticized as a criterion because they may not be within a person's control, and, more importantly, the ends may not justify the means.

Formalism, in which the nature of the action is assessed, can be faulted for the opposite reason: that the means justify the end. The formalist tends to think that if an action is right, then the consequences do not matter; let the chips fall where they may. But willful ignorance of whether the effect of an action is good or bad seems to ignore an important part of the moral equation, especially if the effect is very bad. For example, honesty seems a virtue, but if a man runs up to you with a smoking gun and a wild look in his eye, and asks which way his wife went, it would be best not to tell the truth, but send him off in the wrong direction. If you do not, you could be accessory to murder. A lie to reassure a panicky crowd, or a white lie that saves someone's feelings, may be better than a bitter truth. And we might want to perpetuate the myth of Santa Claus to a two-year old, rather than disillusioning them at an early age by saying, "There is no Santa Claus."

Some people will help others and seem generous, but in the end, they only want to benefit themselves. They want the image of being unselfish but are basically selfish. Outwardly they seem kind but that may be hypocrisy, a disparity between a generous exterior and a selfish interior. Politicians kiss babies, and visit veterans' hospitals, but their motivation could be questioned. The ultimate test is whether a person would continue to offer help even when they are not personally benefitted. Genuine altruists would be giving even when they are not getting, and act for the sake of other people, even at their own expense. Hypocrites want the appearance of benevolence, but always pursue their own advantage. As children they would only share and take turns when mommy was watching.

As was mentioned, people today want something concrete, and therefore favor a consequentialist theory. In the U.S. in particular, we are a practical people, and find the philosophy of Pragmatism congenial to our temperament. The business of America is business; otherwise people avoid the rough and tumble of the marketplace, and retreat to classroom teaching.

Pragmatism is a uniquely American philosophy, associated with the names John Dewey and William James. C. S. Pierce was the founder of the movement in the late 19th Century, and he lays out its precepts in *The Fixation of Belief* and *How to Make Our Ideas Clear.*

According to Pragmatism, we should not concern ourselves with theory, including abstractions about the best type of life. That thinking is "head in the clouds," not "feet on the ground." Theoretical disputes are pointless; it's only practical effects that are decisive. Too much rational speculation has gone on over what ideals and purposes we should have, and the nature of reality and truth. What is I.Q.? Not the folds of the cerebral cortex, or scores on tests, but that which helps us solve problems; there is no "mindstuff."

To the Pragmatist, something is true if it works, if it's useful, not if it corresponds to some external picture of reality. An idea should be accepted when it makes a positive difference in our lives 'True' means what actions will lead to a satisfactory result, how helpful the belief will be to us. Truth is what we will accept as the end of our inquiry. As some psychologists have said, it's time we lost our minds, and came to our senses.

William James, the brother of the novelist Henry James, was an excellent stylist, and made Pragmatism popular outside of an academic audience. It has been said that Henry James wrote literature as if it were philosophy, and William James wrote philosophy as if it were literature. According to a Pragmatic perspective, we should choose "only the expedient in our way of thinking," ideas that have "cash "value." Actions should be praised that are successful, that help us to solve problems effectively.

In *The Will to Believe*, James argues that, apart from the "ontological" question of whether God is real, we should believe in Him because it enables us to live life optimistically. Faith carries with it the belief that we are protected from on high, that prayers are always answered, that life is meaningful, and we will never die. The existence of God is beyond all proof, so we should will to believe because of the benefits it provides. Believing works for us by making life worth living.

James does specify particular circumstances for making such a decision. First, the option must be living not dead; it must be a real possibility to us. For most Americans, worshipping the sun is not a live choice. Second, the option must be forced, in the sense of unavoidable. If our bedroom is hot, we can open a window, or roll over and try to sleep. But we cannot avoid the issue. In effect, not deciding is deciding: we stay in bed. Third, the option must be momentous, that is, important not trivial. Whether our car is blue or grey is relatively unimportant, but whether we support democracy or fascism is consequential.

James maintains that religion is a genuine option because it exhibits all three characteristics. God's existence or nonexistence is live to us because it affects our lives. The decision is also forced. It cannot be avoided but must be confronted. Agnostics, who think the issue cannot be decided, behave as if there isn't a God, so in practical terms, they have chosen atheism. The only, real choice is between believing and not believing. And the decision is momentous in the sense that it is important whether or not we think there is a loving father in heaven or whether we are alone in the universe. Is there a purpose to our being, or are we the result of a chance collocation of atoms? The decision we reach matters.

Obviously, we should believe in God. That belief is justified, verified by its positive, practical results.

Pragmatism suits the American temper because we are a "can-do" people, with "know how" and "Yankee ingenuity," impatient with abstract theories, anxious to get things done, not talk about them. Although we have one of the best educational systems in the world, there is a strain of anti-intellectualism in our national psyche, a populism that believes working with your hands is real work for a grown man. It is agreeable to the American disposition to say that an idea is true if believing it proves successful in our lives.

Just as we should have faith in God, we should also accept its corollary of life after death. To think we will live on in another realm, makes life meaningful, whereas to think the grave is the end, fills us with anxiety and despair. Since there is no certainty either way, we should choose to believe in an afterlife; it makes our disposition sunny and hopeful. We should have confidence that will get our just rewards, if not in this life, then in the next.

The same is true of free will. If we are skeptical, and think all our actions are mechanical, just the product of prior causes, our family upbringing, societal attitudes, and so forth, then we feel powerless and victimized. So, we should believe we are free to choose between alternative courses of actions, to determine the course of our lives. That will induce a sense of power and control.

Pragmatism has been criticized for wishful thinking. Some versions are more rigorous but the emphasis is always on consequences establishing truth. The ends matter more than the means, the positive result not the idea behind it. There is a contempt for objective truth and an emphasis on private satisfaction. As one critic put it, the Pragmatists would have witnesses swear to tell the expedient, the whole expedient, and nothing but the expedient, so help them future experience.

But Pragmatism may be too glib and simplistic. Oftentimes, we turn to a cost/benefit analysis, and outcomes assessment, judge the practical effects of action because that way lies the visible and verifiable. Moral principles are casually dismissed as relative to one's culture, or an expression of individual taste. They are autobiographical comments of the person doing the judging, not about the thing being judged.

But in claiming that Pragmatism is true, the Pragmatists violate their own assumptions, and fail to be consistent. They rely on an outside standard of what is true or false. And Pragmatism would be false if we didn't find it satisfying — which many people do not. We regard truth as something that represents reality, the actual state of affairs. A mathematics teacher does not accept an answer that 2+2=5, even if the student finds it satisfying.

If only Socrates had read William James, he would not have taken the trouble to pursue truth, much less been forced to drink the poison hemlock.

* * *

Judging actions in terms of their worth may be best, even though people today are dubious about objective values. But trusting that some actions are right, and having confidence that we can separate right from wrong, may not be naïve. Instead of thinking of moral laws as written in the sky, or handed down by an all-seeing God, we can identify those actions that contribute to human welfare. As previously mentioned, kindness seems better than cruelty, peace better than war, generosity better than selfishness, equality better than discrimination, knowledge better than ignorance, being part of a community better than living as a hermit, and so forth. There is general agreement among people, and we seem capable of recognizing what is good and what is bad for mankind. This understanding has evolved through centuries of survival and cohesion, so that we know what is necessary for us to live and to thrive.

To make these judgments, we can use the criterion of human welfare, and that is an objective measure. Disagreements may occur over which way is the right way, but through discussion we can reach a clearer understanding of what is best for human beings on earth. As the philosopher Karl Popper said, "I may be wrong, and you may be right, but by a [rational] effort, we may get nearer to the truth."

Ethical principles change through time to some extent, but that does not mean that things like torture were once right, and now are wrong. Rather, that some peoples once thought it was acceptable to torture prisoners or the insane, but now we know better. In the same way, science comes up with new findings, but the truth has not changed. We now know more about the origins of disease, the atomic structure of matter, where the earth fits in the cosmos, and so forth. But we do not assume the earth was once flat and now it is round; rather, that people once believed it to be flat. Similarly, the moon was once thought to be made of yellow cheese, but now that we have walked on it, we know better. Through inquiry, we reach a clearer comprehension of what is so, and that enables progress to occur.

From the "seven heavenly virtues" in the Bible, we might select charity, justice, and kindness, perhaps humility, and temperance. From the "seven deadly sins," we might agree that envy, greed, lust, and gluttony are wrong. Loving one another does seem valuable, and that is highlighted throughout the New Testament. The Bible says nothing about the worth of intelligence, the equality of women and races, or the dignity of man. It does not comment on contraceptives or abortion, or condemn slavery or capital punishment, or say we should respect the natural environment. These are more modern insights.

We can draw up our own list of virtues and vices, and debate their merits, but the standard is the development, thriving, and fulfillment of the individual and society. The conversation is ongoing, but it should be conducted in a rational, open-minded way, attempting to understand which actions are in fact best for humanity as a whole.

6. GOOD AND BAD: RELATIVE OR OBJECTIVE?

Today's fashion is to believe that good and bad, as well as right and wrong are a matter of opinion. Just as in aesthetic judgments, whatever a person believes to be good art, is good art — to that person. The temper of the times is to think that moral judgments are a matter of taste and opinion. No outside standard exists to evaluate anyone's morality, so values are wholly relative, correct only to the person or group that is doing the judging. What's more, values differ between individuals, and between cultures and times, reflecting a variety of perspectives and attitudes, so we can only resolve disputes through compromise, appeal to the courts, or by force. There is no point outside society from which behavior can be judged objectively, no universal values that everyone acknowledges to be right.

Cultural relativism is the name for this position — that values only reflect the viewpoint of different peoples. On this theory, if I say that stealing is wrong, that merely means my society disapproves of stealing; it does not mean there is anything inherently wrong with stealing. Punishment is meted out only for getting caught, for violating the societal rules, codified in law. Stealing, in fact, is sometimes a sign of being smart, more courageous than begging. For spies it is required, a job qualification. And if the theft is done at a high level, by powerful people, they can get away Scot free and be admired for being clever.

In general, it is the society or dominant group that determines what is acceptable. Feminists will sometimes claim that our laws were enacted by men and show a distinct male bias. Because of this, women have been treated as inferior, in business, in institutions, and under the law. Blacks level the same charge against whites — discrimination by the majority. The prejudice of white males is evident in voter suppression, prohibitions against owning property or businesses, resistance to integrating schools, participation in sports. It is not just that the rules are made *by* whites; they are made *because* they are white, and blacks are the victims of the dominant culture.

Subjectivism in ethics is a subset of relativism, for it maintains that values only reflect the feelings or attitudes of the individual. From this perspective, if you say stealing is wrong, that merely means you dislike stealing and wish the other person did too. Sometimes it is called the "boo–hurrah" theory: boo to stealing, hurrah for honesty. In other words, our personal sentiments lie behind our values; they are not objective, or even a function of society, but come about because of our perspective. Different people react in different ways, and we should not criticize anyone for having another viewpoint. Values are individual choices, and we have a right to our opinion. Different strokes for different folks. It all depends on where you sit, how you look at it, your particular standpoint.

Numerous examples can be found that seem to support this position. In ancient, Inuit culture, for instance, the clan would force the very old under the ice, a type of euthanasia, while in Japan the old are honored and cared for in accordance with their tradition. But to the relativist, both societies are right — to themselves. Among the Inuit, the old must be sacrificed if they cannot keep up with the hunting party; it is a matter of group survival. The Japanese need the old as repositories of the skills and wisdom of the culture; their loss would harm everyone.

In the same way, early man was cannibalistic, maybe by necessity, while modern man regards this as an abomination. Western societies enjoy eating beef while to Hindus in India it is repulsive. Insects are delicacies in some parts of the world, and disgusting to eat in America. In many developing countries children are forced to work, while in the developed world there are child labor laws. Slavery is customary in some societies, outlawed in others; drug use is legal in the U.S. (at least marijuana), while it is a crime in Muslim countries. Bikinis are worn on the beach in France, while in Saudi Arabia a woman must be shrouded and sometimes cannot show any part of her skin. Homosexuality is accepted in some nations, and gay marriage is legal, while in others, homosexuality is treated as a capital crime along with apostasy, punishable by beheading. In still others, the death penalty has been abolished as primitive and barbaric. In China blowing your nose in public is rude; "What do you do for a living?" is an impolite question in Holland; showing your teeth when you laugh is offensive in Japan; and being late is expected in Argentina but bad manners in Germany.

In the light of these diverse views, the relativist concludes that morality is a matter of geography and history. Judgments on polygamy, drugs, incest, war, abortion, racism, and so forth, vary enormously across the globe and in various historical periods. Values are determined by the social attitudes of a culture. The joke is that in Italy 60% of men kiss their wife goodbye when they leave their houses; in the United States 60% of men kiss their houses goodbye when they leave their wife. It is a cultural difference.

***

Relativism probably owes its popularity to our present emphasis on tolerance. Today we value multiculturalism, respecting the practices of other nations, and the diversity of our own population. We place the practices of all cultures on a par with our own, and hesitate to believe that America has a monopoly on truth. There is, of course, the doctrine of exceptionalism, the notion that our country is special among the nations of the world, but overriding that idea is a new openness to other traditions. We used to be a melting pot and now we are a tossed salad, more receptive to different ethnicities, sexual orientations, and religious practices, as well as foreign art, music, and literature. Spanish is our nation's second language, and Latino culture is becoming part of our ethos. The country is changing, and soon people of color will outnumber whites in America.

Because of this receptivity toward other cultures, we have lost confidence in our singularity, and are less righteous. The values of other societies might be equally correct, or rather, people wonder whether there are correct values, or only choices by different peoples. With greater awareness of the multiple ways of being in the world, maybe we have to shed our arrogance that "the American way" is best, Increased communication has made us aware of the diversity of values, and we are less confident that we are right in what we think. We do want to retain certain values that seem essential, and constitute part of our nation's identity, such as freedom, justice, dignity, equal opportunity, but that means many other values can be challenged.

In any case, the spirit of the times favors relativism, and sociologists and psychologists tend to agree. *Patterns of Culture* by the anthropologist Ruth Benedict is a paradigm of the social scientific position. In that book Benedict argues that culture accounts for the way people think and behave, including their notion of what is right and wrong.

To illustrate her thesis, she described the customs and institutions of three radically different societies: the Zuni Indians of the American Southwest, the Dobuans who live on Dobu Island off eastern New Guinea, and the Kwakiutl Indians in the northwestern part of the United States

The Zuni Indians are deeply religious — a sober, hard-working, peaceful people, deeply concerned with building a harmonious relationship with nature and the gods. Their whole life purpose is to achieve balance and unity between themselves and their natural environment. The Dobu culture, in contrast, prizes vigilance against the evil that surrounds them. If the people maintain an attitude of suspicion and defensiveness, and regard outsiders as enemies, then they are living sensibly. The Kwakiutl culture differs from both the Zuni and the Dobu by being highly competitive. Personal success, achievement, status, and prestige are of paramount importance, not just reaching a high rank, but being able to look down on those beneath you.

Because of the great diversity between these three cultures, each committed to their own way of living, Benedict concludes that there are no absolute moral standards, accepted by all people, but rather that each culture develops values appropriate to itself. And what is right in one culture can be foolish or shameful in another. A Dobuan male who acted aggressively would be

respected by his culture as a strong man, but Zunis would disap-
prove of him and Kwakiutls might feel contempt toward him for
not seeking distinction. If an individual in the Kwakiutl culture
should succeed in making himself important, this would be considered unseemly by Zunis, and thought childish by Dobuans.
And the Zuni approach to life — the attitude of achieving tranquility, harmony, and peace — would be looked at as pathetic
and puerile by the Dobuan and Kwakiutl.

Furthermore, if we step back and try to judge which society
is best, we would only be reflecting our own culture's values.
No verdict is impartial; no judgment pure and unbiased, and we
certainly cannot evaluate our own society because the principles
we use for judging would be instilled in us by our society itself.

***

The implication of the variety of ethical ideals seems to be
that all values are relative to the culture. No ethical beliefs are
universally held, no judgments of right and wrong or absolute.
One value system is as legitimate as another. It is not that a pattern of culture *appears* valuable to each culture; in point of fact,
it *is* valuable. For the word "valuable" means nothing other than
that which is accepted by a society.

What's more, value systems change over time as a society ad-
justs to new conditions, and responds to different environmental challenges. At one time arranged marriages were the norm,
but now we marry for love (unless there's a pre-nuptial agreement); formerly armies routinely raped and pillaged as part of
the spoils of war, but that is now condemned; pre-marital sex
used to be a social taboo but now it is commonplace; and previously, dominant nations displaced the native peoples such as
the Aztecs, Aborigines, and Indians but now that is criticized
as imperialism. The conclusion is that if values change, whether
with respect to marriage, the conduct of war, sexual mores, the
treatment of indigenous peoples, or whatever, then values are
not eternal. Bibles, codes, and constitutions should be issued in
loose-leaf form.

But before we get too happy about this, we should analyze
the argument. Can we really say that right and wrong are relative because values change through time, and there are diverse
views? Can we legitimately claim that values are invented not

discovered because different people think differently? Do societies create moral principles such as thou shalt not kill, steal, or lie rather than recognizing their importance to human existence? In making an ethical judgment that exploitation is wrong, that sex requires consent, or that freedom is better than slavery, are we just making a personal comment, saying something about our tastes? If we state there should be equal protection under the law, are we only declaring that equality is right because of our society thinks so?

We want to be open-minded, and not condemn values because they are different, but perhaps we need to draw the line somewhere. For example, it is not acceptable for women to be beaten or raped, even if it is part of a country's culture. Women deserve as much respect as men, having the same emotions, perceptions, needs, sensitivities, thoughts, desires, and so forth. Feminist groups criticize Eastern societies for subordinating women, allowing them little education, access to jobs, or freedom of movement. Similarly, genocide should be condemned wherever it occurs. To try to exterminate an entire people is an atrocity and a war crime.

In the same way, stealing property that belongs to someone else is morally wrong, especially if the person earned those goods honestly, through hard work. For a government to willfully take a person's land or livelihood falls into the same category; it is legal stealing. Some philosophers argue that the right of ownership is conferred through labor, and that the thief is appropriating part of a person's efforts in life.

We feel justified everything that preys on poverty, weakness, gullibility, and ignorance. Taking a human life is generally blameworthy, saving a life, praiseworthy, and there are other principles that have become truisms: we should keep our commitments, maintain our integrity, not deceive people, be faithful in marriage, be honest in our business dealings, provide for our children, be loyal to our friends and country, be truthful, reliable, fair, trustworthy, kind, grateful, compassionate, and so forth. In these cases, behavior seems valued because it contributes to human welfare. To say otherwise violates our deepest moral sense.

We want to be progressive and tolerant, but tolerance has its limits. Just as we believe in freedom of religion but we would not invite the Devil into an ecumenical conference. We want to be inclusive, but if we are tolerant toward intolerance, then tolerance would soon disappear.

The main line of defense for the relativist is to point to the multiplicity of moral systems and the changes through time. Across the world each society believes that its viewpoint is right and others wrong, therefore values are relative. But as referred to previously, we should take an analogy with science. We do not assume that all theories are equally correct, so long as a society believes in them. — including the stork theory of birth and denying global warming. And although the findings of science have changed over the years, we do not assume that Ptolemy was as right as Copernicus, that the sun used to orbit the earth but now the earth revolves around the sun. Rather, we assume that people's understanding can be clearer or dimmer, that we are closer to the truth today than people were in the second century of the Christian era. We certainly do not say that because scientific theories change over time, every scientist is only right to himself. Rather, we think there is an external reality and that we gradually gain greater understanding of it.

In other words, what a society accepts does not become correct because a society agrees with it. Instead, we test a society's beliefs against what is actually the case. And this holds true whether we are discussing physical reality or moral values. The alcoholic may value alcohol, the drug addict may want drugs, but that does not make these things good for them, or for their families. In other words, what a person or a society values, may not be valuable. Thinking does not make it so. If people hear voices, that does not always mean that someone is talking to them; they could be psychotic and the voices exist only in their heads. Something is not true simply because we believe it.

The English philosopher John Start Mill makes this mistake in trying to justify his Utilitarian theory — that happiness is the goal in living. In his view, the ideal is to seek the maximum happiness for society as a whole. Mill may be right, but not for the reasons he gives.

He argues that whatever is seen is visible, whatever is heard is audible, and in the same way, if something is desired, then it is desirable. Happiness is something that people desire, therefore happiness is desirable. But even though being seen implies an object is visible, and being heard means it is audible, something desired may not be desirable. In fact, it may not be worth desiring. Driving recklessly or under-the- influence of alcohol or drugs is not a good idea, even if we think so at the time. We are endangering ourselves and others. We might even want to murder a person we hate, but we should not act on that impulse because it violates that person's rights.[1]

Another problem with relativism is that it ignores one of the primary rules of logic: it contradicts itself. For if the relativist argues that everything is relative, that must include the statement that everything is relative, in which case the claim is not true but only relative. That is, it is true to the relativist or his society. And if the relativist asserts that relativism is objectively true, then it can't be true that everything is relative. The only consistent position for the relativist is to say that, relativism is correct for my culture, and to abandon any claim that relativism is true in itself.

Socrates never did get around to reading the Pragmatist William James, any more than Plato was cured of his rationalism by Sigmund Freud, but he did refute his subjectivism. He said the best of the joke is that the person who takes the opposite position and disagrees with you must be right, because everyone is right to themselves. The critic of relativism is therefore right to reject the relativist position. The relativist/subjectivist theory collapses of its own weight.

And under the relativist thesis we could never say that one society is brutal, another more humane. It certainly seems that the Aztecs can be condemned for practicing human sacrifice, the Romans for gladiatorial contests, and in modern times, all sides for the atrocities of war and terrorist activities that continue killing innocent civilians. Conversely, we would never be able to praise the age of Pericles in Greece or the European Renaissance. We could never say there had been progress here, regress there.

---

1 Mill does not say the reverse, that if something is visible it is seen. That would not be true because the dark side of the moon was always visible but it was not seen until a space probe flew by. Neither does he say that if something is audible that it is in fact heard; we know today that Big Bang was audible even though no one has ever heard it.

The cynic will say we have acquired greater knowledge over the centuries but there has been no moral progress or enlightenment; we are only different today, becoming more subtle in our cruelty. We now use chemical and biological weapons, not the thumbscrew and the rack.

But that viewpoint seems too cynical and jaded. Advances have been made in medicine, science, technology, education, politics, art, government, economics, and psychology, the treatment of the old, the insane, the handicapped, the poor, the disadvantaged, minorities, and so forth. Genuine progress seems to have occurred across time and between cultures, and that is only possible if people could imagine better possibilities than that of their own culture.

Above all, we cannot get our minds round to accepting that all judgments are relative, especially when it comes to fundamental values, and that does not seem to be because we are culturally conditioned. Preserving peace and protecting life seem worthwhile for human welfares. Wanton killing, child abuse, sadism and rape, slavery, oppression, and so forth, seem contrary to human good. We can do without psychological guilt, and maybe without feelings of sinfulness, which is a feature of religion, but we ought to retain a sense of moral shame.

7. REALITY AS SELF-CONSTRUCTED

Intellectual history has an anti-intellectual strain that opposes rational inquiry on the grounds that people create their own truth, their personal reality. "There are no facts, only interpretations," Friedrich Nietzsche declares; "There is no truth. There is only perception," Gustave Flaubert writes; and George Orwell states, "Reality exists in the human mind, and nowhere else." The implication is that what is real is our own invention, that the truth is whatever people believe it to be. Something is so only to the individual, a function of their viewpoint, and everyone has a right to their opinion. As Pontius Pilot asks rhetorically, "What is truth?"

In customary usage, reality refers to the state of things as they actually exist, and truth is a property of statements that correctly reflect that reality. However, the above quotations deny objective reality, and claim truth is a function of our personal feelings. There are no warm coats, only coats that keep us warm.

This view was perhaps first articulated in Athens in the 5th century BCE by a group of itinerant teachers called the Sophists, and it has resurfaced at various points in history, including our own times. The Sophists were professional teachers who offered instruction to young people across Greece, and acquired a bad name for being more interested in the fees than in sound instruction. Above the basic education in literature, arithmetic, music, and physical training, the Sophists taught skills in public speaking and success in commerce and politics. They put winning above honesty and far higher than the pursuit of understanding. The Sophists were also known for teaching the youth how to convince others of their viewpoint, using devious but persuasive reasons. They made "the weaker appear the stronger case." For this reason, the word "sophistry" has passed into our language as the use of clever but devious logic to win arguments.

Protagoras is the most prominent among the Sophists, and he is well known for saying "Man is the measure of all things." His fellow Sophist Thrasymachus is reputed to have said, "might makes right"; "justice is the interests of the stronger." Everything depends on power and human judgment, and every belief is true for the person who holds it. If the wind feels cold to me and warm to you, then it is both cold and warm according to the individual. All judgments are subjective.

We know about the Sophists from various sources, including *The Lives of Eminent Philosophers* by Diogenes Laertius, but principally from the Platonic dialogues — the *Theaetetus, Protagoras, Republic,* and *Apology.*

Socrates is the main spokesman in almost all of the dialogues, and he usually gets the better of the argument. For instance, Thrasymachus declares, "Justice is nothing but the advantage of the stronger," that justice for the rulers (the stronger) is to govern in their own interest, and justice for the citizens (the weaker) is to obey the laws that have been enacted. Whatever is desired by those in power becomes just, because that is what they desire, and they have the power to implement it.

But Socrates points out that the laws passed by the rulers may not be in their best interests, that they may be ruling in ways harmful to themselves. What the stronger want, and what is beneficial to them, are not always the same. That means justice, even considered as "the advantage of the stronger," is an independent matter.

To Protagoras' point, that "Man is the measure of all thing," that there is no truth aside from what people think, Socrates points out that the statement is self-contradictory, As mentioned previously, he says, "the best of the joke is, that he acknowledges the truth of their opinions who believe his own opinion false, for he says that the opinions of all men are true."

Skeptical philosophers have appeared throughout history, in fact, they constitute a tradition. In Roman times the Stoics maintained that to defend a proposition as true, you must rely on other propositions as being true, which creates an "eternal regress." They also said that when two claims depend on each other, that creates a circular argument. The skeptic Carneades declared, "Nothing can be known, not even this" and Michel de Montaigne claimed (like Socrates), that he knew nothing, and faith alone brings understanding. Some skeptics, such as the Logical Positivists, argued that specific areas of knowledge cannot be known, such as religion and ethics, but science can be trusted to reveal the world. Some social scientists today claim that scientific truth is only a social construct. Some have denied there is any truth, or if it exists, that it's impossible to know, or that it cannot be communicated.

In the 18th century, David Hume claimed that our most basic beliefs cannot be rationally established, even the belief in space, time, causation, and the self, since they depend upon evidence from unreliable senses. Hume could not maintain this skepticism in real life since, as he said, he would starve to death, walk into walls, or out of windows.

In the 17th century, René Descartes asked how we know whether we are awake or asleep, since dreams sometimes have the vividness of waking life. (And how do we know the difference if we never wake up?) This led to the "brain in a vat" puzzle: that if we were just a brain in a vat, being fed experiences, we would not know we were not living a real life. We could not distinguish these artificial experiences from being in the actual world.

Descartes does acknowledge at least one truth, which is known rationally: "Cogito ergo sum," I think, therefore I am. Whatever I might doubt, I cannot doubt that I exist, otherwise, there wouldn't be anyone there to think or to doubt. We affirm our existence in the act of doubting it.

***

In our present era, Postmodernism is an influential theory —
a re-statement of traditional skepticism, new wine in old wine-
skins. Coming mainly from French academics such as Michel
Foucault, Jacques Derrida, and Jean-Francois Derrida, Postmodernism questions the possibility of immutable and eternal truth,
claiming that there can be no rational framework for knowing.
The framework we use merely reflects our location on the globe
and our place in time, both our geographical position and our
historical situation. Specifically, it reveals our race, class, and
gender, our socio-economic status and the cultural forces that
formed us. This is Sophistry in modern dress.

Postmodernism is characterized by doubt, irony, and irrever-
ence, the rejection of objectivity, progress, science, a fixed human nature, and systems of values. To the postmodernists, truth
is a social construct; objective knowledge, an illusion, and the
theory has been applied to law, architecture, education, politics,
and literary criticism.

In architecture, Postmodernism is a reaction to Modernism, which is seen as authoritarian and exclusive, using rigid
glass and steel materials. In contrast, Postmodernism emphasizes free-thinking, original design that is eclectic, democratic,
ornamented.

In literature it is often called Deconstruction because it fo-
cuses on the contradictions, paradoxes, and fragmentation in
the "text," the unreliable narrator and unrealistic plots. Readers
are made aware that the fiction is a fictional piece, that it has
no fixed meaning in itself but only in relation to the reader and
the words on the page. The meaning of a work can therefore be
understood in various ways, all of which are equally valid.

It is not a stretch to see a connection between Postmodernist
theory and the present tendency to deny all objective truth and
reality. It has had a strong effect on our political life in particular, as well as on news reporting that is sometimes claimed as
competing biases.

***

However, a basic self-contradiction lies at the heart of Postmodernism, an inconsistency that makes us question the validity of the position altogether. The claim that there is no objective
truth must mean that the claim itself is not true in any objec-

tive sense. The statement is self-refuting, and cannot be called true. If it is impossible to know anything for certain, that must include the proposition that we cannot know anything for certain. Succinctly put, you cannot say "There is no truth" is a true statement.

Some skeptics claim that everything we think is the product of our culture and upbringing, which must mean that the claim itself is only the product of the skeptic's culture and upbringing, and not objectively true. On the other hand, if we say that some statements are true, that statement can be true, without self-contradiction.

To elaborate this point briefly, to say that truth is impossible is itself a truth-claim. We cannot know for certain that nothing can be known for certain. And to be a genuine skeptic, we must be skeptical about skepticism. Furthermore, if people create their own reality, they could never be mistaken, but from the fact that people make mistakes, we can see there is an external reality against which beliefs can be measured. Truth seems an objective matter, and not the invention of each individual.

***

Despite the criticisms, many people today speak of versions of the truth, facets and aspects, rather than judging a claim as true or false. People tend to think of the truth as changing and varying according to the period and the culture. What used to be true is no longer the case. Picasso once said that truth must be relative or there could not be a hundred paintings of a tree. (But that might mean painters have different perspectives and styles, not that the nature of a tree changes from person to person.)

It is also claimed that our judgments don't just vary by place and time, but as in relativism, according to each individual's background and perspective, his or her politics, class, religion, race, gender, and so forth. This is the psychological and sociological perspective. Where you stand is a matter of where you sit.

This is the more common form that skepticism takes today. We invalidate a person's views by saying, 'You only believe that because you are a businessman, a Democrat, a truck driver, a Latino, a mother.' It is called "identity politics" and is used Postmodernism to dismiss an idea because of its source rather than judging it in itself. We ignore the biblical dictum "by their fruits ye shall know them," and say "it's by their roots..." . thus, if a member of a legislature favors farm subsidies, an opponent might say, "But aren't you a farmer yourself?"

However, just because the person would benefit from the bill does not mean he or she is in favor of it because of the personal benefit that would accrue. Attacking the person does not address the merits or demerits of farm subsidies. And even if the opposite occurs, and a person is a hypocrite, subsequently accepting farm subsidies after arguing against it, that does not show the argument is invalid.

Some people will claim that wars are fought because politics is practiced by men, a competition for dominance fueled by testosterone. If women had been in charge of governments, the world would be a more peaceful place. Or that because you are from the rural south or Midwest, you dislike cities, especially New York, which you regard as filled with elitist, rootless godless, cosmopolitans. Urban dwellers do not appreciate earning a paycheck by doing a hard day's work. Or because you're white, you can never understand prejudice and discrimination. White people can't teach Black Studies, no matter how informed they are. In order to know, you have to walk a mile in that person's shoes.

Identity politics is also practiced when we want diversity in colleges, juries, businesses, and so forth, not for the sake of fair representation but because various groups are thought to have different truths. It's not that they grasp different aspects of the truth, but truth itself varies from person to person. Then it becomes a rejection of objectivity and a desire to balance out the various biases.

Or else we say, history is written by the victors and so is distorted, even fiction; or that religion only reflects our patriarchal culture, which is why God is considered male. Employees don't know what it's like to have to meet a payroll; or unless you're a Native American, you can't imagine the suffering at Wounded Knee. To know, you must be there, or be part of a people that experienced it.

Feminists will sometimes charge that the laws are made by men, and therefore they elevate men and oppress women. But to say that laws or legislation were enacted by a man does not mean that they were drafted that way *because* it was a man.

In logic this is known as the *ad hominem* fallacy, or an argument against the person, rather than addressing the topic. This can take the form of attacking the circumstances of the individual presenting an argument, for instance, whether a corporate executive or a blue-collar worker, which evades the question of whether what is presented is correct.

In short, our tendency today is to regard truth as subjective, dependent on our personal situation, and not as corresponding to any objective reality. We not only wonder whether a piece of information is true, but question the possibility of truth itself. What's right to one individual may not be right to another, we say; one person's meat is another's poison.

Rudy Giuliani, President Trump's personal lawyer, declared, "Truth is not truth," and that the President could risk perjury if he appeared before the Mueller inquiry because that's only "somebody's version of the truth." In referring to the President's statement that a small inauguration crowd was a large one, Kellyanne Conway, counselor to the President, said it was "an alternative fact." This prompted a comparison to "Newspeak" in George Orwell's dystopian novel, *1984*.

All of this is in opposition to the common-sense view: a statement is true if it corresponds to an actual state of affairs. Something is not true because we think so, but because the claim accurately describes things as they are. When Einstein declared that $E=Mc^2$, he did not add "but, of course that's just me." He believed it represented ultimate reality. Like most people, he thought that true and false refer to what is and what is not, respectively.

Philosophically, this assumes a "realism," the view that there exists an external world, outside ourselves, as contrasted with "idealism," the position that everything that exists is an idea in someone's mind. (Some idealists have even claimed the world is an idea in the mind of God — perhaps a dream, or a nightmare.)

The idea that truth is invented not discovered also has support in academia, for example, from Einstein's theory of relativity applied to other contexts, from quantum mechanics that argues predictability is uncertain, and from postmodernism that distrusts reason and rejects grand theories altogether. It is also favored by social science — especially the fields of sociology, psychology, and anthropology. Each supports the conclusion: that truth-claims do not have any objective validity but are relative to the culture and person from which they spring. But they all cut off the limb on which they sit. They must also doubt their own truth-claims, which are the product of their background.

Of course, the extreme skeptic asks, "Why should we trust reason, 'privilege' it above gut feeling or a sixth sense? But that is an odd complaint, since it questions reason using a rational argument. Maybe the skeptic should grunt and point, since language itself might betray us. Why trust it?

According to a standard of reasonableness, an external reality does exist, and we can measure the truth of our statements against it. Our freedom may not extend to creating reality. We are not as sure of the truth today as we once were, but we still have criteria for distinguishing what is so and not so. Certain ideas are accepted as genuine, and we can trust them until the evidence proves otherwise. Having standards gives direction to our search, and progressive understanding. Without being arrogant, we can have confidence that certain statements are true, others false, and that everything isn't a matter of opinion, that there is a difference between information and disinformation.

8. Is Art a Matter of Taste?

Art is useless aside from decoration, which may not qualify as art at all. Choosing a painting because it goes with the sofa is not an aesthetic decision about the painting. But useless or not, we seem to crave works of art, whether in the form of painting, music, literature, sculpture, theater, dance, or architecture. The well-known cave paintings at Altamira and Lascaux attest to our desire to create and appreciate images, and that desire is present from the beginning of humankind. The cave paintings at El Castillo date from 40,000 years ago.

Commonly, we tell each other that whatever a person likes, is art — to them, that beauty is in the eye of the beholder. It's all a matter of taste, and as the Romans declared, *De gustibus non est disputandum*, about taste you cannot dispute.

But that would mean the paintings in the Louvre do not deserve to be there but only reflect the taste of the curator, that the music played at Lincoln Center is not good music but just favored by the critics, and that Greek architecture is not admirable but merely reflects a style the ancients admired. This subjectivism would throw out works of art that civilization has admired for centuries as merely a personal preference, and not celebrated because of the qualities contained in the art. Rembrandt's self-portraits would be on a par with caricatures or cartoon characters. Is aesthetic judgment a matter of whim, fashion, and idiosyncrasy or is there such a thing as truly excellent art? Are paintings of dogs playing cards, or Elvis paintings on black velvet, really masterpieces if someone thinks so?

Most aestheticians maintain that some landscape paintings, musical composition, or celebrated novel are actually fine works of art, and they debate about the standards that should apply in judging art. How can we declare that a painting of a person's face is beautiful, a still life of fruit in a bowl, moonlight on the water, or time-lapse photography of a rose unfolding? Picasso once said that "truth is multiple, otherwise how could there be a thousand paintings of a tree?" but there could be numerous versions of a tree, some closer, others further away from the truth. Maybe Corot brought out the essence of a tree, and comes nearer to it than a child who paints it as a lollypop.

In the late 1950s and 1960s there was a movement to democratize art, to give power to the viewer or listener, and subvert the authority of the artist, as well as the curator and editor. Associated with the movement were such figures as John Cage, Merce Cunningham, Arnold Schoenberg, Jasper Johns, Robert Rauschenberg, and Andy Warhol. Modern musicians composed works without a tonal center, with no distinction between noise and music, and with enough silence to allow for personal interpretation. Listeners were in charge of judging the piece as dull or interesting. Paintings were created without a visual center or focal point, with strict equality among the elements, and no distinctions were made between entertainment, advertising, and fine art. Warhol painted popular images, of Marilyn Monroe and Campbell's soup cans, eradicating the difference between popular and high culture. Books were published with several endings, so that the reader retained the freedom to choose the most satisfying conclusion. The view was that readers should not be dominated by the author's intentions; power should be placed in the hands of the consumer.

But in this free-for-all, the difference between good and bad art was lost. Some works do seem better executed, more vibrant, and richer than others. Some are more substantial, while others are trivial. The main problem in aesthetics is in separating the superficial from the profound, deciding what justifies the judgment that a work of art is worthy of respect, and should be placed in a museum.

To begin with, we know that a distinction can be made between what we like and what we value. We might enjoy an escapist movie, a horror or adventure film with lots of super-hero action, but in the end, we will admit that it was a bad film. Conversely, we might not like a deep film that leaves us despon-dent and reflective, but be forced to acknowledge that it was an excellent film. And sometimes we like a work for extraneous reasons — because the play has an actor we like, or the scribble drawing was done by our Little Johnny, or the seascape reminds us of that summer vacation in Maine. We are responding to our personal associations.

To call a work of art worthwhile we need to focus on the work itself, and to justify our judgment, with good reasons sup-porting our conclusion. (And in more subtle terms, what we value may not be valuable because we could have bad taste.) We should not praise Picasso's "Guernica" because we dislike vio-lence and it is a political protest against the Spanish Civil War, or value Hugo's "Les Misérables" because we appreciate the set-ting of the French Revolution. Neither should Charles Dickens and Louisa May Alcott be called good writers because they have happy endings.

We must also keep in mind the distinction between art and good art. Little Johnny's scribble-drawing may qualify as art; it is not a bicycle or a tree, and was created intentionally to ex-press his feelings, but whether it is good art is another matter.

***

Over the years aestheticians have developed theories as to what makes good art good, and the principal debate in the phi-losophy of art is over which standard is closest to the truth. The traditional theory is that of representation: a good work of art is one that faithfully imitates its subject. If a painting captures the actual landscape, a story is a slice of life, a bust captures the person, or the music tells a story in sound, then the work is good. Sometimes this is called the mimetic theory, photographic theo-ry, or simply realism or naturalism.

Plato first described it in *The Republic* saying the poet or painter

> can create all plants and animals, himself included,
> and earth and sky and gods and the heavenly bodies
> and all things under the earth and in Hades [by]
> taking a mirror and turning it round in all directions.

Shakespeare repeats the image when Hamlet declares that the end of acting is "to hold as 'twere the mirror up to nature," and Leonardo da Vinci describes painting as "the sole imitator of all visible works of nature...That painting is the most praiseworthy which is most like the thing represented."

On this view, if the artist faithfully imitates people or objects, moods, thoughts, attitudes, or emotions, then he has created a good work of art. As Aristotle remarked, "it is natural to delight in imitation," and children especially like miniatures — toy soldiers, doll houses, tiny cars and animals. We want the representational work to be so accurate that we recognize the object or the person that is rendered, "warts and all."

In ancient Greece, the story goes, a contest was held as to which of two artists could paint more accurately. One of the artists painted a bowl of cherries that was so realistic that birds flew down from the trees to eat the fruit, but when the judges tried to draw aside the curtain to view the other picture, they found the curtain was painted on the canvas; the second artist obviously won; he fooled the judges, not just birds.

Representation is the common-sense view, the response of the person in the street. What the public wants from a picture is that it looks like the thing depicted, not a fragmented image broken up into time frames, or planes of light. If a still-life of a flower does not look like an actual flower, then the average person regards it as a bad painting. The same holds true of dogs and horses, panoramas, family portraits. We use this criterion when we judge children's artwork, praising them as they progress from crude to realistic.

We even appreciate classical music that has a flute duplicating bird songs, the harp for the sound of running water, a cello for the human voice, and trumpets and drums for the noise of battle. Bedřich Smetana's symphonic poem "The Moldau" represents a river beginning at its source, flowing through the countryside, and emptying with a roar into the sea, and when Tchaikovsky's "1812 Overture" is performed, cannons are sometimes brought onto the stage in place of timpani for greater realism in the battle.

When we read a novel, we expect the story to be true to life, the characters and setting believable. We realize it is fiction, of course, and we can only suspend our disbelief so far, but the scenes should come alive. As Marianne Moore said, "The imaginary garden must have real toads in it." The plot should have a natural sequence of events; it should ring true. We identify with the individuals in a story, play, or film, and as Aristotle says, we undergo a "catharsis," vicariously experiencing what they experience, and in the end, feel emotionally purged. This is why tragedy is so enjoyable, even though there might be pain and bloodshed. We empathize with the characters while being protected from the dangers they face, and our anxieties and terrors are relieved in the end. We feel refreshed, as if waking from a bad dream.

Dance, the most ancient art, also represents human experience but by means of a sequence of body movements, usually performed to music, using steps and gestures. Dance can be professional, ceremonial, erotic, sacred, or social, and used to incite warriors to battle or to summon the gods. Figure skating and gymnastics also incorporate dance movements. In general, dance offers a story in mime or interprets the music, expressing and evoking emotion. Dancers cannot speak but use the language of movement, pattern, and choreography to communicate their meaning. The silence itself contributes to the art, making it a purely visual experience.

An example of a simple, representational poem is Longfellow's "The Village Blacksmith":

> Under a spreading chestnut tree
> The village smithy stands;
> The smith, a mighty man is he,
> With large and sinewy hands;
> And the muscles of his brawny arms

Are strong as iron bands.
His hair is crisp, and black, and long,
His face is like the tan;
His brow is wet with honest sweat,
He earns whate'er he can,
And looks the whole world in the face,
For he owes not any man...

It seems to be the representational element that makes us admire a work of art, but that would mean photography is superior to painting since it offers a more exact replica of the subject (although it distorts life since the photograph is frozen, and time never stands still). And what about science fiction, fantasy drawings, or surrealism, all of which are non-representational? What's more, this theory would make painting, literature, and dance more of a skill than an art; they would copy nature, and be a form of plagiarism. Art would be a matter of technique, the ability to draw, describe, or move one's body convincingly rather than the creation of something original.

Also, does the truthful reproduction of just anything in the actual world create good art? If we placed a tape recorder at the average breakfast table, that would probably not make for interesting dialogue in a novel; daily conversation is not the stuff of fiction. Would bathroom scenes make a good play because they're actual, human functions, or would we rather not see that on stage? Would it improve statues to have them skin-colored rather than white marble? A flat, literal photograph taken by an amateur photographer may be dull; ordinary life can be inane and formless. We wonder about Warhol's paintings of Campbell's soup cans or Marilyn Monroe, which was justified as part of our consciousness and therefore worthy of representation. Are there better and worse subjects for art, fit or unfit topics, or is it just a matter of how the subject is treated? Is everything that is natural worth capturing?

Besides, we cannot reproduce the entire, natural world. We must choose a portion of it, and that requires discrimination to enhance interest, an aesthetic principle of selection. The only, truly accurate map of the world would have to be the size of the world. We have all seen statues of perfectly proportioned Greek men and women, but even the Greeks did not look like the Greeks; these are idealized figures with the defects eliminated. Similarly, an author must decide on the events, characters, setting, period, theme, organization, language, and so forth when he begins writing. He or she cannot simply describe reality as it is. Besides, life may not have a plot, no beginning, middle, or end, or contain any purpose, but a novel or short story requires meaning, which implies that life might have to be falsified for the sake of artistry.

Modigliani created stylized paintings of women with elongated faces and necks, as studies in extension and curves; Giacometti stretched his sculpted figures into skeletons, attenuating them to depict loneliness and despair. Even photographers have to decide on exposure, lenses, filters, scale, and definition, and whether to work with still or movie film, color or black-and-white, be purists or use tricks in the dark room, and so forth. Even nature must be composed to be appreciated. We do not take a photograph with a bush blocking the panorama but arrange the scene, perhaps with mountains in the distance, furrows in the foreground, and that cluster of daffodils to the left. The camera always lies, and there is no innocent eye,

In addition, some fields of art do not lend themselves to imitation, particularly architecture. Maybe minarets were invented by cypress trees, houses by cave dwellings, towers by phalluses, and church spires are fingers pointing to God, but by and large the features of buildings are not found in nature. This includes triangles, circles, and squares which do not appear in bare form. Architecture is inventive, and it can produce inspired or grotesque structures, but it rarely copies nature. Buildings are successful or unsuccessful based on the imagination of the architect; doctors sometimes bury their mistakes; architects will build theirs.

In short, art is not a photograph of nature but an imaginative transformation of experience. It can be true to life without being life-like, and it reflects a dialogue between the creator and the subject. Art does not have to bear a resemblance to the world; rather the artist uses his mind and senses to interpret reality. We either respond to his vision or we don't, but we should not judge his work on whether it accurately copies what is real

Representational art appeals to us immediately, but it does not hold up well under scrutiny. Copying is not creating anything original, and nature itself can be more interesting than any reproduction of it. And in selecting what portion of nature to use as a subject, artists will rely on some other criterion besides realism. They will choose what will provide the best affect, even if it means distortion, and select whatever expresses what they want to say.

***

Another theory is that good art is a manifestation of sincere emotions, rendered in a moving way. According to Plato, it "waters the passions," and induces us to accept ideas we might otherwise question (which, to Plato's mind, isn't a good thing). It does not try to understand the world but reacts to personal experience with a discharge of feeling. We see the artist's personality in the work, his impulses and enthusiasms, not the order, decorum, or politeness of society. On this view, art is not an objective presentation of nature but an outward expression of inner emotion.

Art should delight the senses not nourish the mind, otherwise it would be an essay, and its effect does not depend so much on context, but on the emotions that are engaged. We find certain colors attractive — shades of blue or green, for instance, and respond to the texture of marble, wood, water, and skin. We like particular sounds such as the plaintiveness of stringed instruments, the flute, which produces a "white" noise like a boys' choir, or the personal quality of a singer's voice. Even the rhythm and sound of language can affect us — the English word 'memorable,' for instance, the Spanish 'golondrina,' or the French 'coquelicot.' In onomatopoeic words, such as 'buzz,' 'gush,' 'whisper,' 'rustling,' the language mimics the sound it represents. Nonsense poetry uses language without meaning, as in this poem by Lewis Carroll: "Beware the Jabberwock, my son/ The jaws that bite, the claws that catch!/ Beware the JubJub bird, and shun/ The frumious Bandersnatch!"

(Having nonsense words also indicates the mistake of thinking that because we have a word, there must be a reality behind it, that 'angel' and 'demon' stand for actual entities. We also have the words 'Santa Claus' and 'tooth fairy,' but it is unlikely they are real.)

Aestheticians also speculate on whether our responses to sensations are universal or relative to the culture. Does red symbolize something strong to all people — terror, happiness, good luck; is it associated with fire, blood, the setting sun? Does black always mean tragedy and death? In the East white is the color of mourning, but that may indicate a different attitude towards death. Do high notes represent hope, low ones, despair? Do we all like tastes of sweet, sour, bitter, and salty, with the mix varying between cultures? In other words, does everyone respond to physical sensations in the same way, and is it that which we appreciate in a work of art, its emotional effect?

Images also have a strong impact in art, and not just art of a visual kind. We can taste the salt-air in a vivid story of sailing; hear the gong in a painting of a Chinese procession; smell the flowers and feel the breeze in a description of the countryside. Very often, we also experience a bodily response to art. Our pulse pounds, our breath quickens, and we tap our foot, clap our hands, sway and want to dance. In the presence of good art, we also feel a sense of exaltation, a joy and enchantment. We are raised above our common affairs, and realize what existence can be. And through the emotions generated by art, we come away with new insights. Perhaps all great art contains philosophic truths, imaginatively expressed.

Here is Matthew Arnold's celebrated poem "Dover Beach":

> The sea is calm tonight.
> The tide is full, the moon lies fair
> Upon the straits; on the French coast the light
> Gleams and is gone; the cliffs of England stand;
> Glimmering and vast, out in the tranquil bay.
> Come to the window, sweet is the night-air!
> Only, from the long line of spray
> Where the sea meets the moon-blanched land,
> Listen! you hear the grating roar
> Of pebbles which the waves draw back, and fling,

At their return, up the high strand,
Begin, and cease, and then again begin,
In tremulous cadence slow, and bring
The eternal note of sadness in...
The Sea of Faith
Was once, too, at the full, and round earth's shore
Lay like the folds of a bright girdle furled.
But now I only hear
Its melancholy, long, withdrawing roar,
Retreating to the breath
Of the night-wind, down the vast edges drear
And naked shingles of the world.

Emotion does seem a critical part of art, the way roundness is essential to a circle. And emotions can be expressed not just by representation but by an abstract work with clashing colors; in all cases, the perceiver is affected because of the feelings evoked. Unlike sequential time, music presents the generation and relaxing of tension we all experience.

But one question that arises is, "Whose emotions are relevant?" It could be that of the artist, and that what impresses us is his passion, intensity, maybe his obsession. That is, we might be admiring the person behind the work, and since the 19th century there is a romantic view of the artist in his garret, living unconventionally; he will even cut off his ear in a frenzy of emotion. Artists create their art in a trance-like state, at white-hot temperatures, and pour their emotions out on canvas, in paint, words, or music.

Conventional morality does not seem to apply to them because they live a free life, obedient only to their Muse. Even Plato refers to the artist as "inspired and possessed," and Shakespeare groups together the lunatic, the lover, and the poet.

But if the emotion of the artist is what makes art good, then we are not judging the work of art but the person behind the art. Furthermore, awful people can create wonderful art, just as wonderful people can produce banal art. Beethoven, for example, seems to have been a short-tempered, irascible man, but he managed to write nine symphonies that are among the finest ever composed. The state of mind of people can be different than their creation, and the personality of the artist adds nothing to our understanding of the work.

Perhaps it is the emotions generated in the audience that matter most. Here the emphasis is not on the source but on the effect — the fear, desire, grief, hope, joy that the art communicates. Labels sometimes suggest the feeling that the art is intended to convey, for example, "Flowering Garden," the "Pathétique," "Whistler's Mother," the "Emperor" concerto. In any case, if people's passions are aroused at experiencing a work of art, then, on this view, it has achieved its purpose. Indifference is an indication of failure; stimulation means success.

However, this theory would imply that whatever stirs our emotions, or appeals to the largest number of people is good art. No distinction would be made between entertainment and art, pleasure and value; public taste would be good taste, by definition. Patriotic posters, such as those in America during World War II, or Russian propaganda posters depicting the nobility of workers, would be high art, along with sacred music. Bad art would be good if it moved the populace.

However, cheap music can have potency. We know that the works of art in museums are not those most enjoyed by the majority of people, and appreciating good art might be an acquired taste, the result of education. Some societies, in fact, have distrusted art altogether. Goering famously said, "When I hear the word 'culture,' I reach for my gun."

But perhaps it is the critic's emotions that must be aroused. Perhaps. But critics are notoriously unemotional. Maybe they are moved at a deeper level, or control their feelings so as their judgment is not contaminated.

Is it the emotion contained in the work itself that counts? But an inanimate object cannot have feelings. Paint and canvasses lack emotions, and there are no sentiments in canvases, scores, stone, or even words. They are not living things, and exist as means for making a statement, or sharing feelings with an audience.

Who, then, must experience strong emotion for a work of art to be judged good? Because this is difficult if not impossible to specify, the theory of art as emotion may not be the last word.

***

In contrast to these theories, some aestheticians argue that what appeals to us is not copying nature, or strong emotion, but the form of the work, the relationship of elements. It is the proportion, measure, balance, and symmetry that we find attractive. As the English critic, Clive Bell, put it,

> What quality is shared by all objects that provoke our aesthetic emotions? What quality is common to Sta. Sophia and the windows at Chartres, Mexican sculpture, a Persian bowl, Chinese carpets, Giotto's frescoes at Padua, and the masterpieces of Poussin, Piera Della Francesca, and Cézanne? Only one answer seems possible — significant form. In each, lines and colors, combined in a particular way, certain forms and relations of forms, stir our aesthetic sensibilities. These relations and combinations of lines and colors, these aesthetically moving forms, I call 'Significant Form.'

To Bell, each of the arts has formal elements that can be organized in an appealing way. Architecture has features of materials — stone, glass, concrete, steel, marble, and wood; the floors, ceilings, lighting, and stairways; the height of the building in relation to its width; the placement and type of windows and doors, A structure might also contain arches, columns, domes, cantilevers, courtyards, and so forth. The architect must also consider whether the building will appear like an organic secretion of the land, or stand opposed to nature, man flexing his muscles. The composer likewise must arrange his musical elements of melody, harmony, and rhythm, key and chords, tempo and beat, meter and cadence. He must orchestrate the composition by shifting the melody between instruments, the violin, the oboe, the cello, the trumpet, varying the timbre between shades of bright and dark. He must also decide on the form — a string quartet or a symphony, or a concerto, with the soloist in dialogue with the orchestra.

According to a standard scheme, dance uses four elements in its vocabulary: bodily movement consisting of arcs and angles that are sharp or rounded, open or closed; energy which may be strong or light, dynamic or peaceful; space, where the dancers move in straight or curved lines, forward, backward, in diagonals; and time which dictates the pauses and leaps. Classical ballet has rigidly prescribed steps, and the ballerina must seem weightless, whereas modern dance allows improvisation and presses the dancer to the floor under the weight of gravity. In all cases, dance is considered living sculpture or poetry in motion.

Literature, including prose, poetry and plays, uses different elements of meaning, form, theme, setting, rhythm, and rhyme, simile and metaphor, assonance and alliteration. The connotation or emotional association of words is employed as well (the woman will 'faint' not 'pass out,' the sea is not grey but 'wine dark,' and the term 'foot' will be used not a woman's 'feet'). Symbolism is also infused into the text — a lion for strength, a flickering candle for death, a snake for deceit. In literature, everyday language is disciplined and enhanced, used in a more restrained and imaginative way. And sculpture deals with materials, surface textures, forms and space, proportion, scale, and harmony. Sculptors may create their figures using clay, bronze, or steel, taking away the extraneous parts. Inuit sculptors want to liberate the figure that is imprisoned inside.

In order to produce good art, the artist simply combines the elements of his medium into a successful composition. What we appreciate in all art is the pleasing arrangement of the parts. We may be lured by the likeness, but what we value is the composition, with the figures or events as components in the design. A landscape painting is not good because it looks like the land, but because of the relation between the earth and sky, that triangle of rocks against the rounded sun, the splash of green foliage against the blue lake. To appreciate art, we must dismiss the resemblances to any known objects, and look for the abstract form and structure that lies within.

Roger Fry writes,

> In proportion as art becomes purer, the number of people to whom it appeals gets less. It cuts out all the romantic overtones of life that are the usual bait by which men are induced to accept a work of art. It appeals only to the esthetic sensibilities, and that in most men is comparatively weak.

For example, we might respond to the following picture because it resembles a (crude) human face: But the formalist would say that, beneath the surface, we are appreciating the form, and when stripped of its representational qualities, the essence appears as abstract art.

In this view, to ask "What does that painting, or music mean?" is an inappropriate question. The work does not mean but is. It does represent something else but presents a reality in itself, a creation that the viewer can accept or reject as appealing or repelling. It does not mean something different to each person like a Rorschach test, or function like a mirror that reflects the world, but avoids meaning altogether; its aim is to produce a unique, pleasing design, an addition to reality.

It may not even mean what the creator says it means. because artists are unreliable reporters, even of their own creations. As Salvador Dali remarked, "Artists can no more talk about art than vegetables can give a lecture on horticulture."

Haiku with its elegance and economy of expression may exemplify this theory:

> No sky
> no earth — but still
> snowflakes fall

Or the following poem by Emily Dickinson, although the form is atypical and reflects her withdrawal:

> I'm nobody! Who are you?
> Are you nobody too?
> Then there's a pair of us — don't tell!
> They'd advertise — you know!
> How dreary to be somebody!
> How public like a frog
> To tell one's name the livelong day
> To an admiring bog!

"Significant form" is a more sophisticated view of art, less obvious, maybe deeper. But at the end of the day, we have to ask ourselves: Is it the form in a work that makes us appreciate it?

One criticism is that judging a work of art in terms of its structure seems bloodless, sterile, and dispassionate. Composition may be admired but it never moves us, and art that leaves us unmoved is hardly art at all. In analyzing a musical composition, we may notice a rhythmic figure, or that the composition is a fugue with little motifs chasing each other, but although we may recognize these elements, that is not what affects us. If we respond to a melody, it is because it speaks directly to our feelings, not because it is contained in a rondo with an ABACA form. In the same way, we may appreciate a landscape painting, but not because of its spheres, cones, or cylinders. Art seems more of an immediate, visceral reaction than identifying the geometry, analyzing the work intellectually. Content seems to matter more than form.

Also, the arrangement of formal elements matters much more in some arts than in others, as well as in certain styles of art. Literature certainly possesses form but the form counts less than in architecture. Similarly, form is prominent in abstract painting but is less important in representation. And since all art has form (even a dab of paint has an outline), when exactly is form significant? Even modern, atonal music with twelve tone rows cannot escape a pattern. Does significant form consist of diversity or harmonious features. Is it cohesion, integration, and unity or deep complexity?

Significant form is a sophisticated theory, the critic's point of view. It shows a certain contempt for the average person's response. Experts profess to know the hidden reason for the appeal of great art, and how a work affects us. But this may be too precious, rarefied, and ingrown. If it is possible to differentiate between good and bad art, can we trust the aesthetician or critic to make that determination, because they are trained to know?

There is no definitive theory, but the point is that we can argue about our judgments, and try to find the best standards for assessment. The naturalist tries to reproduce life in miniature, the emotivist tells us how he feels about the subject, and the formalist tries to capture the "inscape" of things. Nature does not explain itself, and we wonder which idea is closer to the truth. Nevertheless, we can assume there is a truth to be known. Art is not just a matter of taste, but contains elements that make it worthy of being called good or bad. The trick is to find objective criteria, and the difficulty in doing so should not make us throw up our hands, and say that it all depends on the individual. A work of art should be evaluated in terms of its intrinsic merits.

9. Our Post-Truth Era

The public is used to politicians shading or distorting the truth, and not keeping their campaign promises, but in the present age the deception seems to have reached a new level. Debates always occur as to whether today's excesses are greater or lesser than those in previous times, but at least we can say that many Americans today distrust their government as well as the press. In the information wars, we don't know whom to trust, and that leaves people cynical and disaffected. It militates against social cohesion.

At least we need to be able to rely on the word of our government. Although we are suspicious of politicians, citizens have had confidence that, by and large, their elected officials are dependable, that we can trust their statements. It is especially important to have confidence in one's government in times of crisis, when the public's safety or health is involved. Sadly, this confidence has not always proven to be well-placed.

When a government leader says that a declaration of war is necessary, we need to feel confident there were no viable alternatives, that all peaceful means of resolving the conflict have been exhausted. Gold star families do not want to think the sacrifice of a child, a sibling, a husband or wife was meaningless, but Washington's official justifications for invading and occupying Vietnam, Iraq and Afghanistan have been proven false.

But the ability to trust our government is also important in everyday affairs. Senior citizens need to know that when an official says Social Security funds are safe, they can indeed depend upon receiving their monthly checks. In law enforcement, there must be public confidence that the police officer shot the suspect in self-defense, when his own safety or those around him were threatened.

When mutual trust is eroded, the social fabric begins to tear apart. President George H. W. Bush said, "Read my lips, no new taxes," but he raised the existing taxes, which was a deception. And Bill Clinton said, "I did not have sex with that woman, Monica Lewinsky," when, in fact, he did.

The Watergate Scandal is a conspicuous example of government deception. President Richard Nixon was forced to resign the presidency when his lies and cover-ups of the affair were revealed.

Between 1972 and 1974, during the Republican administration of President Nixon, a break-in was discovered at the Democratic National Committee headquarters at the Watergate complex. The perpetrators were arrested, but the cash found on them was traced to the Nixon Campaign Re-Election Committee. Additional investigations led the House of Representatives to authorize a judicial committee to carry out further inquiries. As a result, open hearings were held during which witnesses testified that Nixon had approved the Watergate break-in and the cover-up, and that audio tapes were available attesting to that fact.

The Nixon administration tried to prevent release of the tapes, but the Supreme Court ruled they had to be surrendered to the Special Investigative Committee. The tapes corroborated the testimonies and disclosed several other breaches of conduct, leading ultimately to impeachment procedures. In addition to the break-in, several of Nixon's opponents had their telephones tapped illegally. The charges against the President were obstruction of justice, abuse of power, and contempt of Congress.

Faced with irrefutable evidence, Nixon was forced to resign from office. If he had not done so, he would have been impeached by the House and removed from office by a Senate trial. Some 69 people of his administration were indicted, 48 convicted, many of them top officials. In his final days Nixon famously stated, "I am not a crook," when he had in fact broken the law and tried to conceal it. The name 'Watergate' has since become synonymous with government scandals over lying and deceit.

Major examples of government untruth include the ever-shifting justification for the recent wars. The Iraq War resulted in the death of 4,424 U.S. military personnel, 40,000 injuries, and 208,000 Iraqi civilians killed. The cost was over $1 billion. Iraq was one of our longest wars, at 8 years 9 months. The Afghanistan War lasted almost 20 years, with casualties including U.S. military personnel, 2,448; U.S. contractors, 3,846; Afghan national military and police: 66,000; other allied service members including NATO allies: 1,144, and Afghan civilians: 47,245. All this depleted the U.S. Treasury by over $2 trillion by the time of our official withdrawal in August 2021.

Officially, the main reason for going to war in Iraq was the claim by the U.S. government that Iraq's leader, Saddam Hussein, had weapons of mass destruction (WMDs). The government also argued that Iraq had ties to al-Qaeda, had conspired with Osama bin Laden to bring down the Twin Towers, and that Hussein was an Islamic terrorist and a threat to the entire region. None of the charges was true.

When C.I.A. Director George Tenet declared there were unmanned aerial vehicles that could deliver WMDs against the U.S., he persuaded many Americans that there had to be a regime change, in fact a coup, and a democratic (i.e., compliant) government installed.

However, inspectors never found any WMDs before the invasion, and none were discovered afterwards. Even if such weapons existed, there were no delivery vehicles that would threaten the U.S. Furthermore, Iraq did not have ties to al-Qaeda.

Similar factual problems have been found with the rationales given for starting many of our recent wars.

Even if some of this relates to misinterpreted intelligence, or selective reading of the information, there is no excuse for making such momentous decisions with so little care, so irresponsibly.

***

More recently, the Trump administration has been repeatedly criticized for uttering untrue statements. In some cases, the statements were mistakes, but in other cases, they were deliberate lies, and with serious consequences. New York

Lies are different than errors, slips, or exaggerations. In *Satanic Verses* the writer Salman Rushdie differentiates between mistakes and lies with a clever anecdote: a mental patient was about to be discharged from an institution, but to be sure he was no longer mentally disturbed, the doctors gave him a polygraph test. They asked him "Are you Napoleon?" The man answered "No," but the lie detector showed he was lying. In other words, he told the truth, but was lying. Obviously, he wasn't Napoleon, but he thought he was.

A lie, therefore, is not something false, but saying what you don't believe to be true. You can't lie inadvertently but only consciously and intentionally. Lies are meant to deceive.

A catalog of such lies has been gathered by various sources, most notably *The New York Times, The Atlantic,* and by Bill Moyers.

Because of the half-truths, distortions, and outright deception by government officials, as well as by advertisers, dishonest journalists, right- and left-wing zealots, and so forth, our time can be called a post-truth era. There is a certain contempt for truth today as something irrelevant. We are practicing the politics that the ends justify the means, which leaves honesty as a casualty in the service of a cause.

* * *

Journalists play a significant role as watchdogs of society. Airing the truth is the best disinfectant. But in the contemporary age, disinformation has become prevalent, in print and broadcast media, and online social media. "Fake news" is everywhere, perpetrated mainly by governments and institutions, disrupting and confusing the public discourse, as well as breeding apathy. It gives power to fringe groups, trades on a declining level of trust in authority and experts, fosters reservations about the credibility of the press and increases the FUD factors: fear, uncertainty, and doubt. Truth-telling becomes not the norm nut an outlier.

The motive behind disinformation is to influence public opinion, and in the case of the media, to expand readership or viewership. This is done by inventing stories about a person or agency — stories that have popular appeal but bear little relation to reality. The ultimate purpose is political or financial gain.

The higher the ratings, the greater the advertising revenues and/ or political impact. This encourages fabrication for the sake of building a larger base of followers.

Special interest groups. especially political parties, will generate false information to persuade people to adopt its point of view. And the public will choose a news outlet that confirms its own opinions, and is willing to accept what is presented as gospel. This is "confirmation bias," an echo chamber in which serious coverage becomes more difficult. Some fake news outlets use algorithms to determine which items to run, and what slant to take, without regard to the authenticity of the information. People become skeptical of news from other sources, and develop a cynicism about the media in general. The news can acquire a reputation for dishonest reporting, a matter of left or right-wing bias, not a presentation of the truth. As the partisan divide widens, and the networks are politicized, the distrust increases. The 'press' and the 'lying press' can become synonymous. Journalists are the gatekeepers of information, but people today question their legitimacy.

It was falsely reported that the Pope endorsed Donald Trump for president, and that Hillary Clinton sold weapons to ISIS and ran a child sex ring from her basement. It is not true that protesters at a Trump rally were each paid $3500, or that Democrats voted to impose Sharia law in Florida.

A new phenomenon is that politicians do not seem concerned at getting caught in a lie; it's no longer embarrassing.

A new technology called "deepfake" can insert any face or voice into a video, and make it appear genuine. We all assume that what we perceive with our senses can be trusted, but we already know from photoshopping, remastering, colorized movies, and dubbed dialogue, that hearing and seeing is not believing. Special effects in film, holograms, virtual reality games, quantum computer simulations, and so on, all make the line very thin between the artificial and the real.

(Philosophers such as Nick Bostrom at Oxford ask whether a conscious mind could live inside a simulation and not know it. This is the "simulation hypothesis" popularized in "The Matrix." How would we know we are inside a video game, if it is never turned off? The same question: how would we know we are dreaming, if we never wake up? Maybe we are all living in a dream — at times a nightmare.)

In politics and supposedly nonfiction information, the use of deepfake is of particular concern. It can be hard to distinguish satire and straight presentations; and politics can easily shift into pure propaganda. For example, in an election in Argentina Adolf Hitler's face was substituted for President Mauricio Macri's, and in Germany Angela Merkel's face was replaced with Donald Trump's. The voice of Nancy Pelosi, Speaker of the House, was slowed down by 25% and the pitch altered, which prompted Rudy Giuliani and Trump, who probably know better, to ask publicly whether something was wrong with her. And the face of comedian Jordan Peele was placed over that of Barack Obama, this time obviously for comic effect.

Counter technology is also being developed, but it can hardly keep pace with deepfakes that go viral and become mainstream. Software tools such as FakeApp and DeepFaceLab are very difficult to detect. Unless there is government regulation, we might reach a point where it is impossible to determine whether a media's content is real.

In March, 2018, the *Atlantic* reported an M.I.T. study, published in *Science* magazine, showing that disinformation on Twitter was being disseminated at a faster rate than true stories. Memes reach more people and at a faster rate than newspapers. It was the largest such study ever conducted, examining 126,000 accounts, tweeted by 3 million users, over 10 years. The conclusion was that "By every metric, falsehood continually dominates the truth on Twitter... Fake news and false rumors reach more people, penetrate deeper into the social network, and spread much faster than accurate stories." Facebook and Google have both made attempts at fact-checking. But the fact-checkers themselves have been accused of lying.

The modern world has become increasingly Orwellian — as in *1984* in which the Ministry of Truth changes the historical record, and everyone must use Newspeak, even though it makes no sense. The cognitive dissonance, and illogicality becomes irrelevant.

In our own age, disinformation is a growing problem and a threat to democracy. A well-informed electorate is necessary for a democratic government to function, and deceiving the public is more characteristic of authoritarian regimes. If, as seems to be the case today, that there is a war on truth, as well as on an independent press, that causes confusion in the electorate and can subvert democracy. It can put someone in office who only pretends to represent the people. Post-truth is pre-fascism.

Various institutions have fought back to protect the integrity of information. UNESCO published a work entitled "Journalism, 'Fake News' and Disinformation: A Handbook for Journalism Education and Training," and the International Fact Checking Network has a code for critical reading and viewing.

The International Federation of Library Associations and Institutions has a checklist for assessing information. The latter includes

1. Consider the source to determine the mission and purpose,

2. Read beyond the headlines to understand the wider context.

3. Check the background of the authors for their credentials and affiliation.

4. Check the supporting data for accuracy.

5. Question whether the piece is serious or meant as satire or entertainment.

6. Ask experts with relevant knowledge for confirmation of the facts.

10. Doing What's Right When It Does No Good

A man enters a hospital for a simple operation, but the doctor notices that he has a healthy heart, liver, and lungs — organs that could save the lives of three critically-ill patients. The doctor decides to end the man's life while he is under anesthesia and to harvest his organs. (An overdose of anesthetics has deniability.) He reasons from a practical, consequentialist standpoint that saving the lives of three people outweighs the good of preserving one.

Most people would regard this decision as outrageous, because even though more people are benefitted in the end, the man's right to life is being violated. As a citizen and a human being worthy of respect, he should not to be deliberately harmed, much less killed, unless he is guilty of some awful crime. What's more, the man has a reasonable expectation that the doctor and staff will act in his best interest.

In short, we would condemn such an act because what is right transcends what is good. The consequences are less important than the principles that ought to generate action.

Ethical principles should determine our behavior, not utility and expediency. Otherwise, what is right is crushed beneath a cost/benefit analysis, and the greater good eclipses all standards. Principled choices should be made, even with little chance of success, maybe even when it does no good. Some decisions do not benefit the majority but do support society's foundations and benefit humanity in the long run.

Perhaps that is the corrective that is needed in our time. The ancient Athenians called it virtue, and maybe Greece should matter more to us than Rome. Perhaps there is an over-emphasis on practicality today, when doing what is correct is more important than immediate benefit.

A distinction can be made between the good and the right. The right refers to correct conduct or behavior, as when we want to do the right thing. Here our efforts are directed at following our conscience and acting as we should. A lawyer might volunteer to represent an indigent man, acting *pro bono*, according to the code of the American Bar Association. He will receive minimal compensation, and his efforts may be wasted because the man seems clearly guilty of the crime. But he believes everyone deserves legal representation, and even if it is a lost cause, the accused is considered innocent until proven guilty. He feels a responsibility to the profession and to ensure that justice is done.

In our age some favor doing what's good, but for the sake of our moral health we need to emphasize doing what's right.

***

Let's take a series of examples:

In an election, suppose a man wants to vote for a particular candidate who he thinks is best qualified for office. However, the candidate does not have the backing of his party, and according to all the polls, does not have the majority of the citizenry behind him. Most likely, he will lose the election.

Should the man vote his conscience or would that be a wasted vote? Would he be a spoiler, taking away support from a similar candidate who would do a decent enough job in office and is more likely to win?

Realpolitik dictates he should be practical and compromise; he should try to elect the good candidate even if he isn't the best. Any other choice is foolish. However, for the good of democracy it might be better if people cast their vote in accordance with their convictions rather than calculating the candidate's chances at winning.

A pharmaceutical company has to decide whether to do research and development of a drug for a small class of children who have a neurological disorder. The drug will have limited sales, and will yield a small profit — if any — but it could mean that a number of children would be able to walk again.

An ethical researcher might argue that, being part of the health care system, the company has an ethical obligation to produce the drug out of common humanity, perhaps using profits from popular medications that bring in high profits. Even though the company policy is that each product must pay for itself, the organization should act according to the ideals of the health profession.

The chief financial officer could counter that their organization is not a philanthropy but a profit-making business. In making decisions, they have to look at the bottom line. Besides, if the sales of the more profitable medications are substantial, that will meet the health needs of many people, as well as increasing employment at the company — both of which are social goods. He has a responsibility to the shareholders, and he would be remiss in his responsibilities if he approved an unprofitable drug.

The researcher could suggest that the more profitable medications could fund the less profitable ones. The company would make a smaller profit but it would hardly go bankrupt, and it would meet the critical needs of children suffering from a debilitating disease. The company is in business to make a profit but that is not its only purpose. Pharmaceutical companies in particular have a wider responsibility to society at large, and not just to maximize growth and profit.

A congressman might decide to sponsor a bill to reduce the inequality in the distribution of wealth. He may believe it is unfair for a few people to have millions of dollars while many are at the poverty level or struggle to put food on the table. He knows the bill will not be popular with his constituents and has little chance of passage in Congress, but the wealth gap is unjust and he feels an obligation to remedy it.

He knows that 1% of U.S. households hold 15 times more wealth than the bottom 50% combined; that middle class income has grown at a slower rate than upper income over the past five decades; that financial inequality in the U.S. is the highest among the G7 countries; that the wealth gap between America's richest and poorest families more than doubled from 1989 to 2016; that the income gap relates to sex, age, race, and ethnicity' and that wealth affects crime, health, and education, as well as family cohesion, opportunity, and satisfaction in life.

If the congressman feels the issue is highly important, his position requires him to sponsor the bill and lobby for it. That is the right thing for him to do, even at the risk of losing the next election.

The manager of a security firm might object to installing surveillance cameras on street corners in high crime areas of the city because it violates the privacy of citizens. He realizes it will help in crime detection, maybe acquitting the innocent, and just knowing you are being watched will reduce crime, but he thinks the price is too high: It is a step toward the state becoming Big Brother, keeping constant watch on its citizens. There should not be an invasion of personal privacy, even in a public space.

He has heard the argument that "If you have nothing to hide, then you have nothing to fear," but that would justify placing cameras even in people's living rooms. Even though they have done nothing wrong, people are entitled to be let alone.

A marketing executive may refuse to use tricky devices of exaggeration, concealment of facts, deceptive packaging, placing important information in small print, using insincere celebrity endorsements, advertising fake free offers and discount sales, and so forth, even though they work. He may choose to persuade people to buy a product by citing laboratory studies of effectiveness, the superior performance of that computer, the test results of that car in acceleration, handling, noise, comfort, and safety.

Lee Iacocca, a top executive at Ford, then at Chrysler, said "Safety does not sell." But that does not mean it should be ignored in the manufacture. Iacocca was also responsible for the Ford Pinto that had a gas tank set too far back in the vehicle. In rear end collisions, the car burst into flames, causing injuries and deaths, but it was cheaper to pay the suits for negligence than retool the assembly line. According to the assessment by the accounting department, it did not pay. For the same reason, the design of the Ford Explorer remained unchanged, even though it was known to have a stability and rollover problem, Because of the cost involved, the company did not address the issue and people died as a result. One woman in California was paralyzed for life and was awarded 83 million dollars in compensation. The court ruled that Ford had full knowledge of the defect but did not want to delay production.

A gun shop owner may insist on background checks and re-fuse to sell assault rifles, whether or not it is permitted by law. He may be committed to the First Amendment but feel that some restrictions are reasonable. He could make more money selling AK47s or an AR15s, but that would endanger public safety. He would not sell a rocket launcher or a tank either, even if it were legal and there was a market for it.

Assault rifles are weapons of war, not for hunting, and peo-ple should rely on the police for protection. The gun shop owner knows that having a firearm in the house is more likely to harm the residents than any intruder. People have the right to bear arms, but within limits, and they also have a right to life and should not be murdered on the street or in mass shootings with assault rifles.

***

We wonder how far people should go in pursuing a lost cause. This is the theme of numerous, poignant films, plays, and novels, a leitmotif of the romantic movement in the arts.

For instance, the classic novel, *Don Quixote* by Miguel de Cervantes, is a major example of fighting for a cause that has no chance of succeeding. The book can be read in many ways, but according to one interpretation, Don Quixote represents a seeker on an impossible quest. He sallies forth as a knight er-rant in search of adventure, in an age far removed from Medieval chivalry. He "tilts at windmills," that is, charges with his lance against a turning windmill, mistaking it for an ogre or beast, and attacks mythical adversaries, always coming out the worse in the battle.

Don Quixote is undoubtedly delusional, taking a wineskin as a giant, some friars as enchanters, an inn as a castle, and a peasant girl as his lady love. But he believes in heroism and gal-lantry and wants his exploits to redound to the greater glory of the knighthood ideal.

However, all his efforts are in vain. No matter how noble and high-minded his sentiments are, they prove fruitless in the end, whether his adversaries are real or imagined. Cervantes paints Don Quixote as both a pathetic and an admirable figure, and the book is simultaneously a comedy and a tragedy.

Another example of a hopeless cause is Ahab's pursuit of the white whale in Herman Melville's *Moby Dick*. With the men of the Pequod sharing his obsession, Ahab hunts the white whale that took his leg. "This is what ye have shipped for men," he tells them, "To chase that white whale on both sides of land, and over all sides of earth, till he spouts black blood and rolls fin out."

The whale symbolizes a variety of things: nature's irresistible power, implacable fate, or perhaps death itself. The "white-headed whale with a wrinkled brow and crooked jaw" could be the incarnation of evil, the destructive part of ourselves that cannot be repressed. That "grand hooded phantom, like a snow hill in the air...shadows forth the heartless voids and immensities of the universe, and thus stabs us from behind with the thought of annihilation." Whatever it means, Moby Dick is inimical to life, and we must struggle to defeat it.

Melville devotes an entire chapter to "The Whiteness of the Whale," white not being a color but "the visible absence of color. "It was the whiteness of the whale that above all things appalled me," a "dumb blankness, full of meaning, in a wide landscape of snows, a colorless all-color of atheism from which we shrink." At the same time, there is splendor in the white of the albatross, the white shark, the white horse.

In any case, Ahab can never defeat Moby Dick but there is nobility in his attempt, and that may be what inspires the crew. In the end, the white whale kills Ahab, and the men on deck see him entangled in the harpoon ropes encircling the whale's body, seemingly beckoning as the whale rises and falls, swimming away.

But we don't have to go to fiction to find examples of admirable but futile actions. Fighting against inequity in wealth may be such a cause today, banning firearms to the public, opposing climate change, trying to make death obsolete by fixing every bodily defect and curing all diseases, through cloning or cryobiology. A square circle is a conflict in terms, so is a rough smoothness, or the whispering silence (although "military intelligence," "pretty ugly," and "piano forte" are only oxymorons). But physical impossibilities may also exist, although they may not be known beforehand. Should Sir Lancelot have gone on a quest for the holy grail, and should we pursue ideals?

The phrase "lost cause" is often used by Southerners about the Civil War, where they saw themselves as fighting for a way of life, even though their struggle was doomed. They did exceptional things, which made them exceptional people. They went to the front lines with a "forlorn hope," even though they were conscripted, and only wanted to get back to their fields and family. Clarence Darrow said, "Lost causes are the only ones worth fighting for," and that sentiment made the South feel victorious in its defeat.

Following a military code, soldiers have given up their lives to do their duty, out of patriotism for their country, even when they knew they would not succeed in their mission. These are heroes, who are not regarded as foolish but remarkably brave, celebrated nationally. In some cases, they knew they would die, but felt honor-bound to continue to fight, not to secure victory but to fulfill their duty to their country. They felt called upon to do what is right, even though it did no good.

Christian martyrs did not think they were throwing away their lives pointlessly. Some thought that if they added "the stubborn ounces of their weight" to a holy cause, the heathen would be converted, but some persisted even when they knew their efforts were futile. The Catholic Church even has a patron saint of lost causes, St. Jude, who spread the message of the Gospels in the face of great adversity and certain death.

Are war heroes throwing away their lives uselessly if they know the enemy has overwhelming forces and superior weaponry, when all hope is lost? Are martyrs foolish in embracing crucifixion, to die as Christ did, if no one is brought to God by their example? It is a thin line between foolishness and bravery, between pathological compulsion and rational commitment. And the courage of these individuals can be put down to chemistry — an adrenalin rush or a dopamine high, or psychologically, a group hysteria. It might even be a death-wish that makes them fight to the end, which would certainly qualify their sacrifice.

But it does seem that some people, who are healthy-minded, will risk their lives for national, moral, or political beliefs, and a few will give the "last full measure of devotion." Some dedicate their lives to God, not for the sake of winning heaven but to carry out his purpose on earth.

Short of the extreme of self-sacrifice, acting morally may be superior to intending to do what's right, or judging an act by the good it achieves. In the latter case, a person never knows what to do but only what they should have done, in retrospect. And we do not have to throw up our hands and rely on situation ethics. An objective judgment can be made in terms of human welfare, and that will certify which actions are right. A principle is validated by the value that it contains for the body of humankind.

11. CHARACTER AND DUTY

As mentioned previously, right refers to actions that are ethically correct, usually in terms of specific rules of conduct. Ethicists might, for example, defend the value of honoring commitments, being honest, or preserving human life, and condemn cheating, lying, and stealing. Or they might approve of keeping our word, respecting property, or being kind and generous, and condemn acts of murder, theft, and adultery.

Religion too has its set of right principles and moral laws, from the Code of Hammurabi in Mesopotamia (1800 B.C.E.) and the Eightfold Path of Buddhism (c. 520 B.C.E.), to the Ten Commandments and the Sermon on the Mount. Usually the "thou shalt nots" dominate the list, greatly outnumbering the "thou shalts," which is unfortunate since prohibitions can create a taste for that which they prohibit. From a psychological standpoint, positive reinforcement does more to alter conduct than negative reinforcement.

Those who follow this ethic claim that actions are right according to their value for humanity. For that reason, we must accept them as obligations in our lives. An act is not right by virtue of its outcome, that is, by the fact that it promotes some good result, but because of its inner moral quality, and once we recognize this, we realize that the act should be done, regardless of whether good or bad will come of it. The emphasis is on our duty to perform certain actions, apart from their outcome. We are responsible to behave in moral ways, not to achieve positive ends, acting according to the value of the act itself. If we do so, our existence is justified.

Doing what is right has the advantage of focusing on conduct, not on the agent's intention, or the subsequent result, and it uses as its standard the moral nature of the act. If conduct is correct, in terms of its value to human life, then the motive and the consequences are beside the point. Helping others, for example, might be regarded as ethically correct, and no subsequent consequence could make it wrong. If we help an old lady into a taxi that later is involved in an accident, that makes no difference in the moral equation; we did the right thing, and could not control or foresee what would happen. A correct action remains correct even if it turns out badly; some ethicists would say, even if the right thing is done for the wrong reasons.

Those who endorse the right, consider certain acts right apart from societal norms. Saving lives, for example, might be considered right, even if one's culture thought otherwise because human life is worthwhile in itself, not sacred because it was given by God but worthy of respect. An act is sometimes difficult to separate from the motive or result, but insofar as it can be separated, it constitutes the main component of morality. Furthermore, most advocates of the right, treat rightness as universal. That is, if certain acts are truly right, as perhaps promoting the dignity of man, then they should be practiced everywhere and always. If cheating is wrong in the United States in the 21st century, then it is equally wrong wherever it occurs, in all other historical periods. If drunkenness is a wasted life now, it is a wasted life elsewhere. In short, that which is, in fact, right, is universally so; it cannot be right for one person without being right for all.

Some moral philosophers endorse the good over the right, meaning that an act should be judged not by its nature but by its outcome. Whether there were beneficial or harmful consequences is the critical question in making moral judgments.

According to this school of thought, what someone actually accomplishes is the relevant factor, not how a person behaved. If, for example, Affirmative Action were motivated by a desire to remedy racism but, in fact, produced a backlash against African Americans, we could not say it was a valuable program. This is one charge that is made against the invasion of Iraq that inflamed the Middle East, even if that consequence was unintended. If an act begins in benevolence but ends in violence, then the act is wrong and its moral purity cannot redeem it.

Good people can do a great deal of harm, so moral worth should be determined by consequences alone. For this reason, Deng Xiaoping cited the Sichuan proverb: "It does not matter whether the cat is black or white as long as it catches mice," and the Bible declares "by their fruits ye shall know them."

The term 'good' is also used in a non-moral sense, as when we refer to a good watch, a good tree, a good dinner. Here the term 'good' means that the object functions efficiently or is excellent in its qualities. As G. K. Chesterton said, "If a man were to shoot his mother at a range of 500 yards, I should call him a good shot but not a good man."

Objects are value-neutral; they have no ethical quality in themselves. Our moral judgments regarding objects have to do with the use to which they are put. An axe can chop down a tree to make baseball bats, furniture, or a violin, or it can be wielded by an executioner to chop off heads. A buoy can save lives by marking a safe channel, or cause death if a boat should collide with it and capsize. Nuclear power fuels the sun, and its energy can heat and light homes, or it can be used as a terrible weapon in war. The examples are endless, but the point is that things are neither good nor bad. Axes, buoys, nuclear power, or even alcohol, drugs, or guns cannot be categorically condemned as evil; it all depends on how they are used.

***

The difference between the two approaches can be illustrated in our criminal justice system. The reasoning behind the incarceration of a criminal can be either because it is right or because it is good. That is, a sentence can be handed down according to the severity of the crime, where the aim is a fair response for wrongdoing, just retribution. Perjury and minor fraud, for example, should be lightly punished while armed robbery and kidnapping deserve stiffer sentences; murderers might be executed as a matter of justice.

If people are imprisoned for thirty years for a trivial offense, common sense dictates they have been unfairly treated, but if a serial killer receives a sentence of six weeks in prison, that also violates our sense of fairness. When the punishment fits the crime, in the sense of being proportional to it, then we believe that justice has been served. We use language such as, "A debt to society has been paid," "The criminal received his just deserts," or "The person got what he had coming." On this model, justice means an equivalence between crime and punishment; the person received the penalty that he deserved.

In a cosmic sense, it is as though the equilibrium of the universe has been restored, the scales of justice had been balanced. This is the foundation of the Old Testament idea of an eye for an eye and a tooth for a tooth, which was thought just in the sight of God. By saying this, the ancient Hebrews did not mean we should retaliate with the same action, that robbers should be robbed or rapists raped, but responding in kind, that is, in direct proportion to the seriousness of the offense. It is a balanced, measure-for-measure morality rather than a vindictive feeling, that society should get even for an offense against it. In its pure form, this approach represents fairness; in its corrupt form, it may mask a desire for revenge.

In punishment theory, this approach is called *retributive*, for the hallmark of justice is fair retribution. There is no thought of the effect that the punishment might have on the person or society, but only the correctness of the punishment in relation to the offense. It is backward-looking not forward-looking, because punishment is meted out as a reaction to the crime. Because John did X therefore, he should receive Y, not in order to reform him but to give him what justice demands.

In contrast, a *utilitarian* theory of justice (small 'u') is based on the good that it hopes to achieve. A criminal is punished in order to bring about a positive result, both for him and for society Under this model, the punishment is intended to reform and rehabilitate the offender so that he or she will not repeat the offense. The severity of the punishment does not depend on the nature of the crime but on what is needed to change the person's behavior.

The punishment is also aimed at deterring others from committing similar crimes by showing what will happen to them if they do. An example is made of the offender which, it is assumed, will have the effect of discouraging people from committing similar acts. In addition to reform, rehabilitation, and deterrence, criminals are imprisoned so that society will be protected from them; they are paroled or released when they are considered safe. Until that time, they are disabled, rendered harmless. In pronouncing sentence, the judge considers the time necessary to bring about reform and rehabilitation as well as what is needed to deter potential criminals so society is protected.

The punishment is thus apportioned not to the crime but to the desired effect; the crime only serves as an index of the type of sentence that is needed to reclaim the person as a productive member of society. Since it is forward-looking rather than backward-looking, the main concern is the beneficial consequences of the action.

If, then, a bank robber is sentenced to ten years in prison because that is considered appropriate to the crime of grand larceny, a retributive theory of justice is being used. If, however, the ten-year sentence is given because that is the time that is considered necessary to reform and rehabilitate the criminal, to protect society and to deter potential criminals, then a utilitarian theory is operating.

One point is worth noting here. Although the utilitarian theory appears to be more liberal, enlightened, and humane, this approach has a serious weakness. Namely, it could be used to punish people who have not committed any crime. For if a psychological profile should show that someone is dangerous, or if society needs an example as a deterrent, then people could be sent to prison even if they are innocent of any offense. The retributivist theory may be too close to vengeance to make us comfortable, but at least it ties punishment to crime; at least punitive measures are taken because someone is guilty of unlawful conduct. In utilitarianism, punishment need not be connected to any crime, thus making it potentially unjust and dangerous.

***

The 18th century philosopher Immanuel Kant is considered among the eminent philosophers. He presented a celebrated theory of ethics in his *Foundations of the Metaphysics of Morals* and the *Critique of Practical Reason.*

Kant espoused an ethic of right, of duty and character, as well as emphasizing the importance of a person's intention. Nothing in the world ... can possibly be conceived which could be called good without qualification except a good will, Kant writes. It is the will behind an action that matters, the motive of the agent performing the action. A person of good character, someone with "a noble nature," is praiseworthy — regardless of whether his or her actions actually achieve some beneficial result. Circumstances, chance, accidents, and so forth may prevent the accomplishment of what a person wills, but such obstacles are morally irrelevant. The significant factor is whether the intention of the person is pure. If so, then praise is appropriate, and if not, then no praise should be given, regardless of whether the action proves beneficial.

But for the will to be good, Kant stipulates that it must operate out of a recognition of a moral duty, not from inclination. For example, if we were moved to help a blind person because of a sudden rush of pity for his condition, that would not constitute a moral action, but if we offered our help because we recognize that everyone has a duty to help the handicapped, then the action would have a moral character. Kant distrusted the emotions, regarding them as fickle, too unreliable to determine what's right. The emotions could induce acts of sympathy and generosity but they could also impel us to cruelty and destructiveness. Just because we have certain feelings, that is no reason to act on them, and that applies to kindness as well as cruelty. But if we realize that certain acts are morally binding on us, then we have a firm basis for action.

The next question for Kant was how are we to know what is right, where our duty lies? We might accept the notion that obligations rather than emotions are the foundation of morality, but how is one to determine which actions are moral? Kant answered by saying that if our act can be subsumed under some general principle of conduct, then we know we are in the realm of morality. If we can say that a contemplated action is an instance of some general rule of behavior, we can feel confident in proceeding. For example, suppose we are contemplating the rightness of stealing rather than earning money by working. Maybe we are disgruntled about the unequal distribution of wealth and feel that blue collar workers get too small a slice of the pie, the C.E.Os. a disproportionately large one. In order to test the morality of stealing, we must ask ourselves whether such an action could become common practice. Could we in good conscience recommend that everyone steal money instead of working for it? Obviously not, for if no one produced, there would be nothing to steal. The action does not fall under a general principle and is therefore wrong.

Kant sometimes described this standard of morality as "respecting the moral law." By this he meant operating according to objective rules of rightness in contrast to behavior that springs from emotions or is based on the consequences of action. "Duty is the necessity of an action executed from respect for law...," Kant wrote.

Kant formulates this view of correct conduct in what he called the *Categorical Imperative*. Various descriptions are given of it, but the rule can be stated as follows: We should act in such a way that the principle for our actions could become a universal law. That is, in order for an action to qualify as moral, we should be able to say that all people at all times and all places should do likewise.

He elaborated his categorical imperative by saying that if we cannot declare that everyone ought to do what we have done, then we know our conduct is wrong. When we make an exception for ourselves, declaring that the action is generally wrong but we can do it anyway, that is a sign that our action is immoral. A genuine rule of conduct has no exceptions. If the rule can be applied to everyone, then we know the action is right.

Kant gives various examples of the operation of the categorical imperative. Suppose we are considering borrowing money, but in order to obtain the loan we must promise to repay it — which we do not intend to do. Should we make an insincere promise to repay the debt in order to obtain the loan? To decide this question morally we must apply the categorical imperative. Could we will that everyone should act according to the same principle, that whoever wants to borrow money is justified in making a false promise to pay it back? Of course not, Kant says, for if everyone did this no one would ever lend money. The conduct cannot be universalized and therefore is not right. The same is true of suicide. If everyone committed suicide, there would be no one left to practice the value of committing suicide.

Another example is that of truth-telling. In some circumstances, we may be tempted to tell a lie, perhaps to extricate ourselves from an awkward situation, or to spare someone's feelings. But the acid test of the rightness of our behavior is whether it extends to everyone. Can we will that everybody should lie? Apart from negative effect on society of a general distrust, Kant maintained that lying would be impossible to universalize, for if everyone said the opposite of what they believed to be true, then no one would ever be deceived. Universal lying, then, would be self-defeating, which means that lying is wrong.

Kant did not say that a maxim could be considered wrong if universalizing it would be immoral; rather that it cannot be right if universalizing it would be impossible to carry out.

To take still another example, Kant says, it would be impossible to have a contract with four clauses specifying the mutual obligations of the parties involved, and a fifth clause stating that either party could break the contract whenever he or she wishes. Such a contract would negate itself, and cease to be a contract at all. In the same way, any principle that contradicts itself when universalized is thereby revealed as being outside the realm of rationality and morality.

Kant formulated the categorical imperative in another way that seems quite different from the concept of universalizability, although Kant regarded it as essentially the same. The *Practical Imperative* states "Treat humanity, whether in thine own person or in that of any other, always as an end and never as a means only." Kant is here emphasizing the dignity of human beings, or, more specifically, rational beings, and affirming that people should not be used merely as instruments or objects. Notice that Kant says "as a means only," thereby acknowledging that people must regard each other as means to some extent, whether as employers, shopkeepers, mothers, or doctors. But human relationships ought to be more than that. We should, Kant believes, regard people as worthy of respect in and of themselves, and treat them as the ends of action not as a means for achieving some aim.

This version of the categorical imperative provides a second reason for condemning stealing, suicide, cheating, and lying. In all cases we are treating someone only as a means. With regard to deceiving another person about our intentions to repay a loan, we are using him in order to secure money. This is the reason why we feel humiliated when we discover that someone has lied to us; we have been regarded as obstacles rather than persons. In the case of suicide, we are treating ourselves as a means of escaping our problems, and ignoring the respect that should be accorded to all human beings, including ourselves. Kant's analysis may seem odd, but when suicide is condemned, whether by the church or some other authority, the argument is that taking a human life is wrong, and that means our own life as well as the lives of others.

Treating humanity as worthwhile is an important element in Kant's ethics, but his theory hinges mainly on the concept of universalizability, which is the main formulation of the categorical imperative. It is only if we can claim that the rule behind an action can be applied to everyone, that we have a duty to perform the action.

***

But is Kant correct? Can we accept his categorical imperative as the fundamental touchstone of morality, the way to conduct our lives?

When we analyze the Kantian position, a problem that strikes us is the difficulty in finding any universal principle. For example, it might be right to keep our word but some promises should never have been made, and should not be kept. A woman has no obligation to stay with a man who abuses her, even though she promised "in sickness and in health, 'til death do us part." In such a case, loyalty would be misplaced, and leaving the person would be the right thing to do, out of self-respect. Here, we do not have a responsibility to be loyal, to finish what we started. Or we may believe in the value of human life, even its sanctity, nevertheless we could justify killing in self-defense, to protect our life or those we love. Not long after Moses fetched the Ten Commandments down from Mt. Sinai, he was engaged in a bloody war, yet the Fifth Commandment says, "Thou shalt not kill." The rule, therefore, can be broken; it is not universal, and is not right.

Considering the numerous exceptions to rules, it seems impossible to defend any value as being right at all times. We are told that promises should be kept, but we are not obliged to return a package entrusted to us when we find that it contains drugs or explosives. We may believe that stealing is wrong, but if we are starving because of an unjust political system, then stealing food might be justified (as in *Les Misérables*). Or we may have been raised to think that violence is evil, but if we are in a political situation where the worst people hold the best people in a state of subjection, then a violent revolution might be justified. We also accept truthfulness as a value, but we would not want to give bad news to a woman with a weak heart if the truth could kill her. Here we would have a moral duty to lie, and to do so as convincingly as possible.

There seems to be a problem, then, in finding any principle that can be applied absolutely, without exception. Only universal rules as truly right, but we cannot find any rules that are universal. Even though we do not approve of stealing, lying, breaking promises, and so forth, there can be extenuating circumstances in which we feel obliged to do so. By insisting that only those principles without exceptions are moral, Kant created an empty system, one without any principles that satisfy the criterion. The standard is so high, that nothing qualifies.

Setting aside this problem, another objection to Kant's system is that two universalized principles can conflict. Suppose, for instance, we maintain that human life should be preserved and also that we should always tell the truth. Then one day a man with a smoking gun in his hand and a wild look in his eye asks us which way his wife went. In these circumstances we can either tell the truth, and be accessory to murder, or protect a life by telling a lie. We are forced to choose, because we cannot both preserve life and tell the truth. Many moral principles contradict each other in this way, and the dilemma cannot be resolved under the Kantian system.

It might be argued that, in this case, we can decide which of the two principles takes priority, and set up a hierarchy of values with the most important at the top. Preserving life seems weightier than telling the truth, so it should be given preference. But people will go to the wall for the truth, holding it higher than life itself. It is part of the quality of life, and quality may be more important than quantity.

The preservation of life seems to be the overriding consideration, but situations could arise in which other values would take precedence. A doctor, for example, is bound by the Hippocratic Oath to both preserve life and alleviate suffering, and that can pose a conflict. For instance, in the case of a burn victim, who is terminally ill and in extreme pain, a doctor might decide to forego "heroic" measures to prolong the patient's life, for that would mean prolonging his suffering. Euthanasia might be more compassionate and courageous than letting the person die a painful death.

The same problem, of finding a rule that cannot be overridden, plagues us whenever we try to establish a ranking leading to the highest moral principle.

In addition, some principles might be moral even though they can't be universalized. For example, self-sacrifice does seem commendable at times but it cannot be practiced by all people at all times. For if everyone were constantly self-sacrificing, there would be no one left to accept the sacrifice. On Kantian grounds, therefore, we would have to reject self-sacrifice as a virtue. Nevertheless, sometimes it could be worthwhile. For example, suppose someone were starving to death and we were well fed; then we should sacrifice our meal and give it to the starving person. The point is that an action need not be universal in order to be moral; it can be moral in particular circumstances.

Conversely, some principles can be universalized even though they are not moral. For example, the rule that we should exploit the weaknesses of other people for our own advantage does not contradict itself when it is universalized. It is possible for people to constantly take advantage of each other's weaknesses, but that does not make for an ideal society. The fact that exploitation is capable of being universalized does not legitimize it.

Kant's overall mistake has to do with right actions having to be universalized, as expressed in the Categorical Imperative. He fails to distinguish between qualifying a rule and making exceptions to it. That is, it seems legitimate to claim that we should not make an exception for ourselves in affirming a moral rule;

that would be self-serving. But Kant takes this to mean that a moral rule cannot have qualifications. Granted that it would be wrong to argue, for example, that "No one may break a promise except me," nevertheless, that is not the same as qualifying promise-keeping by saying that "No one may break a promise unless a person's life would be endangered by keeping it." In the latter case, the qualified rule might be universalized without exceptions, which would satisfy the criterion of the categorical imperative. By failing to make this distinction, moral rules become stricter and narrower than they need to be.

Oddly enough, one weakness in Kant may be ignoring the virtues of results. In his eagerness to avoid the defects of consequentialism, he throws out the baby with the bath water. For to judge actions solely in terms of their nature, without regard to their results, can make us callous to human suffering. Kant said, for example, that if a sentence of death were just it should be carried out today even if we knew the world would end tomorrow. It is similar to John Wesley's statement that "I would not tell a willful lie to save the souls of the whole world. " It might be worth telling a lie if that would save the entire world. And maybe we should not execute a person, even a guilty person, if there were no one left to benefit by the example. This type of thinking, which dismisses consideration of the effects of actions, can maintain principles at the expense of people. Kant's ethical system has been described as, "a cold-hearted moral machine."

One final point: if, for example, we should violate our principles of preserving life and go to war against an aggressor nation, we are not implying that killing is right but only that in some cases it may be permissible. Killing is still wrong and preserving life is still right, but we can sometimes override that principle for the sake of the greater good.

Therefore, people who say that killing is sometimes right, are misstating the point; taking human life is always wrong, but it may be allowable in certain circumstances. What is right should not always be done, and what is wrong is sometimes allowable.

Recognizing this, some later thinkers made a useful correction to the Kantian system. Maybe there are no universal duties, but there might be *prima facie* obligations. That is, some values are *apparently* right, and should be followed. These might be actions conducive to human welfare. They are not universal obligations, or innately right, but they can be seen as generally worthwhile. "For the most part," "by and large" they should be followed, for the well-being of humankind.

Kant's ethical theory, although seriously flawed, is an intriguing and persuasive one, perhaps because of its purity. In some fundamental way, it seems appropriate to say that actions are intrinsically right, and that an intrinsically right action should always be done, that whatever can be proven to be a universal obligation is thereby correct.

12. Pleasure As the Goal in Life

When people ask themselves what they are living for, many will answer that they just want to be happy, meaning that they want to enjoy themselves, to maximize their pleasure in life. This is the most common idea of success in living, and it seems a natural way of thinking. From our earliest days we tend to identify the pleasant life with the good life, an enjoyable experience with a desirable one. When children say, "The candy is good" they mean it is tasty, thereby making an equation between what is pleasurable and what is good. We use 'good' in the same way when we refer to a good vacation, a good party, or simply a good time. (As mentioned, there are other meanings of 'good,' as in a good car, good music, good health, or good fishing.)

What's more, pleasure is an ultimate end rather than a means toward some further goal. We do many things in order to be happy, but we are not happy in order to obtain anything else. It would be odd to ask people why they want happiness, or what they hope to gain from it, because happiness is never a way to achieve something else; rather it is a goal for which other things are done. As Aristotle pointed out, our enjoyment is self-sufficient. Once we have attained it, we do not need anything else besides; it is complete in itself, without gaps. If we lack something, we are not fully enjoying ourselves, but if we are in a state of enjoyment, we lack nothing. Since happiness is self-sufficient, that qualifies it as the ultimate good.

Other factors also incline us to accept the idea of happiness or pleasure as our goal in living. For one thing, both pleasure and pain are regarded as simple feelings, incapable of being reduced to more basic terms. In addition, the individual who experiences pleasure considers it to be good, while the person who experiences pain regards it as unequivocally bad. Some good things may result from suffering, but that does not mean the suffering itself is good; we would just as soon have the positive without the negative. Finally, it seems that all acts considered good have some element of pleasure connected to them. If pleasure is a common denominator, again it would appear to be our fundamental goal.

These are some of the reasons given for a commitment to pleasure. but in a more basic sense, most people take it as a "given." That is, it seems so self-evident, that it hardly requires justification. We simply assume that an enjoyable life is a good life.

This affirmation of pleasure (or happiness) is called *hedonism*, and it is one of the oldest theories in ethics. During its long history, various types have been developed and distinguished. Psychological hedonism is the doctrine that human nature is so constituted that people cannot help but pursue pleasure and avoid pain. In Freudian psychology this is called "the pleasure principle." It is not a matter of what people ought to do but with what people must do; not what should be sought but what in fact people desire. We simply have an instinctive drive toward pleasurable activity.

As a theory of human behavior, it is not, strictly speaking, a part of ethics but a description that has implications for ethics. The psychological hedonist claims that all animals, including human beings, automatically seek pleasure and avoid pain. This is a universal law of nature that has no exceptions. Pleasure is the prime motivator of all activities, and people who say they act for any other reason are only fooling themselves or deceiving others. All alleged altruism is basically the pursuit of enjoyment for oneself, even if the agent pretends otherwise.

Psychological hedonists claim to see through the pretenses of human conduct. People who give money to a beggar are not moved by concern for the beggar's welfare but by the satisfaction they will receive from this (outwardly) generous act. This is reinforced by the thought that few acts of philanthropy are secret; most generosity is displayed for public approval, thereby increasing the pleasure of the agent. For example, a charitable gift to a foundation usually bears the name of the benefactor, just as a donation to a college does. Campus buildings will carry name of the benefactor, and so does the scholarship fund. In the case of charitable giving, the psychological hedonist claims the donors are basically increasing their own self-esteem. They will think themselves superior to the beggar, the charity, or the person they have helped, and the fact that others are obligated to them, only increases their self-satisfaction. In general, the gift has increased their pleasure, and maybe diminished their (liberal) guilt. It was because they anticipated this result that they responded as they did. To give is not only more blessed than to receive, it is much more gratifying.

To the cynic, all actions that claim to be performed for the public good can be explained in a similar way. Doctors do not enter their profession from humanitarian motives but because of the wealth and status they will derive from it. Parents who sacrifice for the good of their children do so because of the pride they will feel in their accomplishments. Religious people do not seek to serve God hut hope to gain the respect of their neighbors, and divine protection for themselves — in this life and in the life to come.

But this viewpoint may be overly skeptical. Many activities seem to be carried out without any hope of reward or pleasure. We often act out of habit or distraction, or for the attainment of certain ends. It is true that pleasure may be the result of achieving those ends, but that does not mean it was the motive. Those people who give a dollar to a beggar may derive satisfaction from their generosity, but it is doubtful that they helped the beggar in order to feel satisfaction. It seems more likely that they responded to visible suffering. The psychological hedonist may claim that firefighters, who risk their lives to rescue people, or martyrs who are burned at the stake, or soldiers who volunteer for a dangerous mission, are motivated by the ultimate pleasure they will feel, but there is little proof of this. In fact, the evidence seems to go the other way. A person driving a car, who has a choice between crashing into a tree or hitting a child, might choose the tree, risking his own life. The driver could not have given any thought to the pleasure to be derived from saving the child.

To look at the matter slightly differently, people seek various goals and when they reach those goals, they feel a certain satisfaction. But satisfaction is not what they are seeking; rather, it is a result, or byproduct of the achievement. Pleasure might he an emotional tone that accompanies the experience, but it is not what the person is seeking.

Enjoyment, then, is not the implicit or explicit aim of all actions. Therefore, it seems a mistake to say that human beings are motivated to seek pleasure, much less to say that they are never motivated by anything else.

***

Ethical hedonism is far more interesting and significant. This type of hedonism does not maintain that people must pursue pleasure, that it is a law of human behavior, but claims that we ought to seek pleasure. Ethical hedonists are not interested in describing what people do, but in prescribing what they ought to do. To their minds, pleasure should be the goal in life.

Ethical hedonism is sometimes based on psychological hedonism in that pleasure is considered to be natural to human beings and consequently desirable. In other words, ethical hedonists will sometimes claim that since people naturally pursue pleasure, they are therefore justified in doing so. But even if desiring pleasure is natural to us, that does not mean it is worthwhile; sadism and masochism might be natural to us as well. And it makes no sense to advise people to do that which they cannot help but do. We never suggest that people should breathe air, since they must breathe air in order to live. In the same way, it is pointless to recommend the pursuit of pleasure if pleasure is all that people can pursue. We might be pleased about it, but we cannot advocate it. Commending is not the same as recommending.

But ethical hedonism need not be founded on the psychological variety. Ethical hedonists can say that, regardless of whether people do pursue pleasure, they should pursue pleasure as the good in life. Even if people are capable of seeking other goals, pleasure ought to be chosen.

One important distinction that can be made within ethical hedonism is between individualistic and universalistic varieties. The individualistic hedonist maintains that pleasure (or happiness) should be pursued — but only for the person performing the action. Trying to bring enjoyment to others is useless because we never really know what will satisfy people; it is difficult enough to determine what will please ourselves. Human desires are so varied and strange that it is impossible to predict someone else's taste. If we offer a man a glass of wine, we may find that he is a Moslem and we have offended him. If we offer a guest a soft bed for the night, we may discover that he is an Indian fakir and would have preferred a bed of nails. And if a man opens a door for a woman, she may be a feminist who regards the gesture as patronizing.

But even if we could determine what would bring pleasure to other people, the individualistic hedonist sees no reason why we should do so. Our sole concern should be to obtain pleasure for ourselves. If we forfeit our own enjoyment in life for the sake of someone else, we will have missed life's greatest blessing, and there is no reason to make that kind of sacrifice. If each person takes care of himself or herself, society as a whole will benefit; if we interfere in each other's affairs, even with the best of intentions, we will probably make the other person miserable. This is reflected in the laissez-faire doctrine of the economist Adam Smith who thought that an "invisible hand" regulates the marketplace, so as individuals pursue their private gain, the society as a whole is enriched. A free-enterprise system is best, not a society of self-sacrifice.

Universalistic hedonism stands in sharp contrast to the individualistic kind. Rather than advocating that individual pursue their own pleasure, universalistic hedonists recommend that we pursue pleasure for society as a whole. This is an altruistic doctrine not a self-interested one. All of our actions should be directed toward the maximization of enjoyment for everyone, not just ourselves. Our own pleasure should count as much as any other person affected by our actions, no more and no less. We are only one in the moral equation, neither privileged nor expendable. If bringing pleasure to others increases our happiness, then so be it, but that is not our purpose; it is only an accidental outcome.

Universalistic hedonists do not believe in either the selflessness of Christianity nor in the selfishness of individualism. Their concern is with the well-being of humanity altogether, with each person considered an equal part of the whole. Our attitude toward actions should always be "Will this increase the total amount of happiness for everyone?"

On the surface, it is difficult to separate the individualistic and the universalistic types because both will help other people. But the motive for individualistic hedonists is to increase their own pleasure through helping others; their generosity reflects well on them, and is a means toward increasing their personal pleasure. The universalistic hedonist, on the other hand, helps others for their sake not his or her own.

Since the motives behind actions are invisible, it is hard to separate them in practice, but one way of differentiating between the two is to see whether the person would continue bringing pleasure to others even if it meant displeasure to them. Those who persist would be universalistic, not allowing the reduction of their own enjoyment to keep them from pursuing enjoyment for all. Those who stop at the point where providing pleasure to others did not bring pleasure to themselves, would be individualistic.

***

From a historical perspective, a man named Aristippus was probably the first self-declared hedonist, and he endorsed the individualistic version. He studied under Socrates in Athens before diverging from his master's sober rationalism. Subsequently, he started a school at a place called Cyrene on the coast of North Africa, and his followers were referred to as Cyrenaics.

Aristippus held that all good is determined by pleasure, and more specifically, that pleasures that can be enjoyed in the present are far superior to any that we can remember or anticipate. The pleasures of the past or the future are pale shadows and cannot compare to the experiences we enjoy in the knife-edge instant of now. In one of his surviving fragments, Aristippus wrote "[the moral good] has nothing to do with the recollection of past enjoyments or with the hope of future ones."

Not only did Aristippus feel that momentary pleasures are best but, as a corollary, that we need not pay much attention to the duration of pleasures. The fact that our enjoyment might be transitory or fleeting, does not detract from its worth; we should try to get as many beats into the given moments as possible, and that means that each pleasure must be brief.

Furthermore, the Cyrenaics argue, we should strive for maximum intensity in every pleasurable instant. The stronger the experience, the more desirable for the individual. Tranquil, sedentary, passive enjoyment are weak compared to the intense satisfactions available to the humans. In addition to feeling that immediate pleasures of a brief and intense kind will produce the best life, the Cyrenaics also maintained that the pleasures of the body or senses are more desirable than those of the mind. The joys of eating delicious food, drinking wine, making love, lounging on the beach, the feel of the sea, and the sun, are far better than mental contemplation. The intellectual pleasure of learning, the companionship of friends, the mellow contentment of art, music, or literature, pale in comparison to vivid sensuality. Aristippus made no distinction as to better or worse pleasures; he was solely concerned with how intense, physical, immediate, and intense our experiences were. One way of living was not better than another, only richer in the amount of pleasure it provided.

This is essentially a *carpe diem* philosophy, an "eat, drink, and be merry" approach, that is uninhibited. Enjoy what you can today and do not look back on a golden past or hope for a wonderful future. Live life to the fullest, taking from the present moment all the joy it contains, and the more intense and physical your pleasure, the more satisfying your time on earth will be.

The Persian poet Omar Khayyam, although not a Cyrenaic, expressed the Cyrenaic philosophy in his poem *The Rubaiyat*:

> Come, fill the Cup, and in the fire of Spring
> Your Winter-garment of Repentance fling:
> The Bird of Time has but a little way

To flutter — and the Bird is on the Wing...
A Book of Verses underneath the Bough
A jug of Wine, a Loaf of Bread — and Thou
Beside me singing in the Wilderness –
Oh, Wilderness were Paradise enow!...
Ah, make the most of what we yet may spend,
Before we too into the Dust descend;
Dust into Dust, and under the Dust to lie,
Sans Wine, sans Song, sans Singer and — sans End!

Or as Edna St. Vincent Millay put it centuries later,

My candle burns at both ends
It will not last the night;
But ah, my foes, and oh, my friends —
It gives a lovely light.

Appealing as this philosophy might be, certain embarrassing difficulties began to emerge that coalesced into a formal criticism of the Cyrenaic philosophy. First, if we simply take advantage of pleasures available now and do not look ahead to what might happen in the future, we might pay dearly tomorrow. For example, if we want to maximize our pleasure in drinking, to intensify the experience as much as possible, we will find ourselves sick the next morning. Or if we want to indulge ourselves in eating, gorging ourselves whenever we can, we will find that our body becomes overweight and unhealthy. Heart problems could follow.

There is also the opposite problem of refusing any momentary discomfort because we are not sure it will provide future comfort. That attitude can be equally self-defeating. There is a story about a Greek boy who was carrying a bag of gold, and, because it was heavy, he threw it away. This is short-sighted and most likely, he would come to regret that impulse at some later point. If we decide in haste, we might repent at leisure.

Wisdom dictates that some immediate pleasure ought to be rejected because they are going to lead to subsequent pain, and some immediate pain should be accepted because of the rewards they offer in the future.

Enduring some pain at the dentist might be worth it.

In addition, intensity might not be wholly good, in terms of what could follow from it. For the more we increase the intensity of our pleasures, the more likely it is that an opposite will follow. The higher the wave, the deeper the trough; the higher the mountain, the deeper the valley (and the "slough of despond").

For example, suppose that a man wants to increase his enjoyment of speeding in a car and drives at 90 miles per hour, then 100, then 120. The chance of having an accident increase proportionally; the faster he drives, the more likely it is that he will lose control of the car and crash. Or imagine trying to maximize the experience of sky-diving by opening the parachute later and later; the longer the jumper waits, the greater the thrill — and the danger. Not pulling the rip cord at all could be a "rush," but it would be a short-lived pleasure. The same holds true for taking drugs. If people progress from marijuana to heroin, they will certainly accelerate the "high," but they run the risk of addiction, of ruining their lives and dying an early death. As we increase the intensity of our experiences, we escalate the likelihood of pain, whereas if we lead a more tranquil life, the negative consequences tend to be milder.

And if intensity is not worthwhile, the value of brevity is also questionable, because the Cyrenaics accept brevity mainly in order to maximize intensity. One cannot have a long intense experience but only a brief intense one, so short pleasures are the price the Cyrenaics pay for having strong ones. But if intensity is not necessarily desirable, we need not put up with a brief experience; all things being equal, we would prefer enjoying our pleasures for as long as possible.

Finally, we can challenge the notion that the pleasures of the senses are the most satisfying kind. Some philosophers argue that mental enjoyment is richer and deeper than momentary sensual pleasures. As one critic wrote, "It really shouldn't surprise us that the pleasures of the moment are only momentary pleasures." The satisfaction of mental states might be preferable to those of the fleeting, superficial, and animalistic pleasures of the senses.

Because of these problems, a series of modifications were made to the Cyrenaic theory, which culminated in a different type of hedonism altogether called the Epicurean school.[3] The philosopher Epicurus who founded the movement and gave it his name, lived in Athens following the death of Aristotle. We know that Epicurus studied Plato's system and the ideas of pre-Socratic philosophers such as Democritus. We also know that he taught in Asia Minor before he founded his institute of philosophy in Athens. Here, he conducted classes on paths in a walled garden. The garden of Epicurus became as famous in its time as the Academy of Plato or the Lyceum of Aristotle.

Epicurus took as his goal in life achieving a serenity of the mind and the comforts of the body. Anything which disturbed an individual's peace and tranquility had to be avoided. In fact, Epicurus thought it was more important to avoid pain than to pursue pleasure. In his thinking, a neutral state is most desirable, "the absence of pain in the body and of trouble in the soul." The overall aim is to keep ourselves in a serene state. The Epicureans criticized the Cyrenaics not only for pursuing excitement but for concentrating only on immediate experience instead of the total amount of happiness in life overall. If we are only concerned with physical pleasures in the here and now, we may find that our lives are generally miserable. There should be a long-term balance of pleasures over pains, and this involves a good deal of rational thought, of deliberation, and foresight. We have to assess pleasures to see which ones will not be negated by subsequent pains, and which pains are worth enduring for the sake of subsequent pleasures. Therefore, an intellectual approach to experience is necessary. It directs our activities, tempers our passions, and ensures a pleasant life as a whole.

Because of this emphasis on rational control, the Epicureans began to stress the happiness that the mind can provide over the pleasures that the senses yield. It is the intellect that is most important, both in controlling our activities and receiving higher enjoyment. By seeking mental happiness, we avoid intensity and look for peace — which is much safer in the long run. We not only avoid the temptations of immediate enjoyment that is, the pleasures near at hand, but we also avoid the temptation of choosing the intense experience over the more harmonious one. With the mind in command, we can choose peaceful modes of enjoyments that are of long duration rather than risky, brief ones, and because they are extended, they can be deeply satisfying. What we should seek is a placid state of consciousness.

As noted, Epicurus regarded pleasure basically as the absence of pain. To him, the good life consists in avoiding suffering as much as possible and not seeking positive pleasures in an active way. If we can maintain ourselves in a condition that is not painful but comfortable, then we can say we are in a good way. In this state of mind and body we are serene.

The walled garden of Epicurus has always been taken as an appropriate symbol for the philosophy because it was a retreat, sanctuary, or refuge where people could escape from the struggles and vicissitudes of the world; they could live a life of undisturbed enjoyment. Walls, of course, are ambiguous: they keep things in and keep things out, and it is a matter of emphasis as to which is primary. Epicurus' garden wall was clearly intended to keep problems at a safe distance, outside.

There was something of the monk about Epicurus rather than the saint or martyr, for he did not dedicate himself to the welfare of others but led a secluded life in the service of a personal ideal. For a hedonist, his life was unusually ascetic and modulated, and he encouraged his followers to practice an equally austere and disciplined existence. Sumptuous food, intemperance, and riotous living were all condemned, and a diet of bread and water was thought sufficient sustenance, with a moderate amount of wine on feast days. A person's residence was to be modest, and economically furnished to satisfy basic needs, and the daily routine was simplified to include only essential activities.

Epicurus affirmed the value of friendship for the gratification it would bring rather than for the sake of the friend, and sharing a meal with others was encouraged: "To feed without a friend is the life of a lion and a wolf." The body too had to be cultivated, not for clarity of mind, or any spiritual transcendence, but to maintain the health of the organism; sickness should not disrupt our tranquility. Exercise and proper rest were essential, but not a regimen of athletic training to win honor at the Olympic Games. Only enough care of the body was necessary to keep it from plaguing us.

The Epicurean way of living, then, favored moderation throughout, the regulation of sexual passion, the control of bodily hungers, and the continual monitoring of sense gratification. Epicurus tried to move the center of our being from body to mind, from excitement to quiescence, from active to passive states, and from thrilling moments to a mellow state of contentment.

It would seem as though the Epicurean type of hedonism is an advance over the Cyrenaic variety, but it might not be wholly good. By seeking to avoid pain rather increase pleasure, Epicurus and his disciples adopted a negative attitude toward life. In essence, they were retreating from the world, turning inward and choosing a protected, secluded existence. This attitude can be characteristic of old age when people want to be left in peace; they no longer look for risk or excitement. The same and familiar are preferred to change.

The Cyrenaics by contrast are vital, positive, and spirited. They want to take chances and affirm existence, saying yes rather than no to life. To view the world the way the Epicureans did would eliminate all spontaneous and impulsive action. And we are not at all sure that intensity should be avoided because there could be painful consequences, any more than we think that tranquility is a blessing simply because it will be followed by more tranquility. Passion may be worth the price.

The Cyrenaic philosophy is a young person's attitude toward life, stressing the pleasures of the body that are immediate, intense, and momentary, and although this approach may not be wise in an Epicurean sense, nevertheless it can yield a better life than the careful, prudent attitudes of later life. To be reasonable in all of our decisions does not bring much joy, and the adultness of the Epicureans can be chilling; it can be a truth that kills.

It is uncertain, then, whether the Epicurean theory is an advance or a retreat in hedonistic ethics. Both the Cyrenaic and Epicurean theories have their merits, and we might think it best to combine the two in a compromise. However, this is difficult if not possible, because their characteristics are opposed to each other. We cannot, for example, have brief enjoyment of long duration, or an intense tranquility. Venturing may be incompatible with centering. We might want to vacillate between these alternatives, choosing to be Cyrenaic when young and Epicurean when old, or divide the two between summer (Cyrenaic) and winter (Epicurean), play and work, night and day, but it is hard to build a consistent life this way. As Aristotle said, to hit the bull's eye we must know the target. Besides, to attempt a pleasing mixture, extracting what we regard to be the merits of each, is really choosing an Epicurean approach, that is, a balanced life.

Both theories have a self-centered, individualistic character, and this has troubled ethicists for some time. The Cyrenaics desire physical pleasures of short duration that are immediate and intense, but they want it only for the person. The Epicureans seek extended, tranquil, mental happiness in life as a whole, but they too want this for the individual. Neither one adopted a universalistic ethic of altruism, or seemed concerned about injuring others, so long as the action promoted personal enjoyment. Epicurus spoke for the Cyrenaics too when he wrote, "No one loves another except for his own interests," and "Injustice is not in itself a bad thing but only in the fear, arising from anxiety on the part of the wrongdoer, that he will not escape punishment." In other words, injustice might disturb our tranquility, or our sleep.

This pursuit of individual enjoyment also lays hedonism open to a criticism called the hedonistic paradox. This paradox, quite simply, is that pleasure or happiness cannot be obtained directly, but comes about as a side effect or by-product of the pursuit of other goals. For example, people who strive for self-realization or to serve God, may find that they are happy in their dedication, but people who deliberately try to be happy find that happiness eludes them. Happiness or pleasure seem to be attained indirectly, and are destroyed when they become the goal. It is like trying to fall asleep, when we can only fall asleep when we stop trying, or turning on a light to see the nature of darkness. Any attempt to enjoy ourselves is self-defeating, and the pursuit of happiness seems an unhappy pursuit. Hedonists are faced with the further paradox that. by preaching happiness as the goal in life, they are decreasing the likelihood of people attaining it.

One philosopher, John Stuart Mill (discussed below), made this concession in his *Autobiography*: "Those only are happy who have their minds fixed on some object other than their own happiness.... Ask yourself whether you are happy, and you cease to be so.... Treat not happiness, but some end external to it, as the purpose of your life...and if otherwise fortunately circumstanced, you will inhale happiness with the air you breathe."[5] This appears true, but it undermines the hedonist theory.

Other criticisms of hedonism center on the idea of "false happiness," that is, happiness based on illusion. For example, a husband might be pleased to think that his wife loves him when, in fact, she does not. A boss might believe that his employees are happy with his leadership when they actually find him lacking. If people live in a fool's paradise, they may be happy, but it is a happiness based on fantasy, and not worth having.

In the same way, electrodes could be inserted into "pleasure centers" of the brain, which are then stimulated. That does not seem genuine happiness, any more than the chemically induced euphoria of drugs such as Ecstasy or crack.

There is also the problem of "wrongful happiness." Wealthy people might enjoy having a number of houses, several boats, and exotic vacations, but suppose they acquired their wealth through fraudulent means — by cheating customers or shareholders, for example. Is enjoyment worthwhile that comes by dishonest means, and is undeserved? The sadist or masochist, the voyeur or exhibitionist might find their life pleasurable, but that does not justify it. Maybe we need to have executioners, but we hope they don't enjoy their work. Similarly, the Germans have a word 'schadenfreude,' which means finding pleasure in someone else's misfortune. Such pleasures may not be worth having.

Considerations of this kind make us wonder whether pleasure is good in itself, or whether it is dignified enough to be the goal of human existence. Enjoyment seems a part of a good life, and it is hard to call life good without it, but it also seems cheap and sometimes covers a multitude of sins.

Still, as Homer wrote in *The Odyssey*, "Dear to us ever is the banquet and the harp and dances, and changes of raiment, and the warm bath, and love, and sleep."

13. PURSUING HAPPINESS FOR EVERYONE

The theory of hedonism had its advocates in ancient Greece and Rome, but it did not undergo substantial changes during the Middle Ages or the Renaissance. In Medieval times religious devotion became paramount, and enjoying life suspect. The Catholic catechism states that the purpose of life is the glorification of God, not the pursuit of happiness.

Some development did occur in the 17th century at the hands of the English philosophers Thomas Hobbes and John Locke, but significant work was not done until the 19th century when Jeremy Bentham and, subsequently, John Stuart Mill gave hedonism a new emphasis. Both men advocated theories of universal happiness, not just for the individual, developing a social hedonism that they termed Utilitarianism. The end of action had to be an increase in the overall pleasure and happiness of society, and they conflated pleasure and happiness as the components of the general good.

The principle of utility, which forms the core of the utilitarian ethic, maintains that we should seek "the greatest amount of happiness for the greatest number of people." In other words, we should not seek pleasure or happiness for ourselves alone, but for humanity in general, and this happiness should be as great and extensive as possible. The rightness of our actions can be measured by whether they made the majority of people happy.

If so, our conduct was praiseworthy; if not, it was blameworthy. Success in living was gauged by the extent to which we rendered the lives of our fellow man enjoyable.

By seeking "the greatest happiness for the greatest number," the Utilitarians were being altruistic, promoting a humanitarian doctrine. In contrast to individualistic hedonism, their orientation was–the happiness or pleasure of society at large. The Utilitarians considered the agent performing the action as one among those affected by the action, not counting for any more or any less than anyone else. It was not a matter of sacrificing oneself for the good of others. or putting oneself ahead of others, but of treating one's own happiness as having an equal claim beside that of everyone else.

Jeremy Bentham was the first hedonist to advocate a utilitarian position — an English philosopher and social theorist who was interested in political reform; he wanted to increase the well-being of all social classes. Bentham was also impressed by science, which was emerging in his day, and he thought he could apply science in the service of ethics. He wanted to bring about an increase in the social good through the scientific application of social principles. To Bentham's mind, ethics had been much too vague, ambiguous, and imprecise in the past, but the time was ripe to introduce scientific rigor and exactitude into ethical thinking.

Since Bentham was a utilitarian, he was interested in scientifically determining the amount of happiness that any action would yield, and he thought this could be quantified and precisely measured. To do this we had to know the extent to which various activities yielded happiness, and we needed to establish which of two actions would provide more happiness for more people.

With this in mind, Bentham devised what he called the hedonic calculus, felicific calculus, or calculus of pleasures — a scheme for scientifically measuring the amount of pleasure or pain any action would yield. He thought that he could reduce pleasure to certain "hedons," that is, units of pleasure or pain, capable of being added or subtracted. Furthermore, he wanted to isolate each of the factors that were involved in pleasure and pain, and to rate actions according to the number of hedons that they provided.

Bentham isolated the factors involved in conduct, and re-duced them to "seven marks." *Intensity, duration, certainty, propin-quity, fecundity, purity,* and *extent,* (the number of people to whom it extends). Bentham assumed that these seven marks were an exhaustive list of the characteristics involved in the attainment of pleasure. He also believed that he had culled the best hedonis-tic thinking from the past.

Having isolated the relevant elements, Bentham used them in his hedonic calculus. The seven marks are applied to any given action, and the sum of hedons might be determined, for example, according to a scale of +5 to -5. The same process would be car-ried out with regard to pains. Then the negatives would be sub-tracted from the positives to see whether the act was pleasur-able overall. If the result proved to be positive, then the act was shown to be enjoyable and should be carried out, but if there was a negative result, the act was shown to be largely painful and should not be performed.

One criticism that can be leveled against the calculus relates to its universal aspect. As a utilitarian, Bentham should be very concerned with the number of people affected by a pleasurable action, yet the factor of extent is only one of seven marks in his system; that is, it counts as only one-seventh in the total cal-culation. If Bentham had made extent weigh more than any of the other factors, or perhaps more than their total value, then a utilitarian result would be more likely. But as the calculus stands, it does not guarantee that an action which touches more people will turn out to have a higher number of hedons than one that affects fewer. In his eagerness to construct a scientific ethic Bentham seems to have betrayed a fundamental principle of util-itarianism — that of "the greatest number."

In Bentham's defense, he believed society as a whole would be made happy by each individual pursuing his or her own hap-piness. But this is willful blindness since there can be conflict between the happiness of the individual and that of society. A better approach would have been to place more weight on ex-tent, rather than assuming that the individual's happiness would automatically enrich the whole. For example, if a company pollutes the environment to increase profits, that may increase the wealth and happiness of the owners but it does not increase the happiness of everyone. Adam Smith's "invisible hand," that claims individual gain will automatically produce public wealth, cannot be counted on.

Is it true that whatever we do for ourselves, benefits other people? Not necessarily. Sometimes what helps us, harms others. Is it true that whatever we do for others, will benefit us? Again, not necessarily. Sometimes generosity does not return, and may not even spread outwards. Good deeds are not always rewarded, nor do they return benefits to the person; what goes around may not come around.

A second major problem with Bentham's calculus of pleasures has to do with the specific numerical values that are assigned to each factor. There seems to be a lot of imprecision in the number of hedons that are awarded. If an experience promises to last an hour, should it be given a 3, 4, or 2 in duration? If an action brings pleasure to five people does that mean it is worth 1 or 3 in extension? In comparing two actions, the problem is not so much deciding which action should be given a higher number of hedons, but knowing how much higher. For example, downhill skiing is certainly a more intense experience than perch fishing, but is it twice or three times as intense? The problem comes in trying to obtain an exact measurement of something as amorphous as pleasure, and for the calculus to work, precision is required. With a change of only one or two numbers, an alternative action could be indicated as best in the final arithmetic.

The general problem comes down to the fact that pleasure is not amenable to quantification. Bentham attempted to apply numbers to something that eludes exact measurement. With regard to states or feelings, there simply cannot be a numerical assessment, a moral arithmetic. Bentham's system breaks down because of this, and seems artificial and strained. In the last analysis, the hedonic calculus is unreliable as an instrument for determining happiness. It is not on the same level as differential calculus or integral calculus.

We also wonder about the moral aspect of Bentham's theory. That is, by relying on maximizing pleasure as the criterion for conduct, we could endorse an immoral act that provides more pleasure over a moral act that yields less. An action that yields pleasure to the majority is not necessarily moral, for that pleasure could come at the expense of the minority. We have examples of this in the raucous crowds that attended public executions in earlier times, the massacres of rival races, tribes and religious groups around the globe, and so on. Perhaps one might posit that the pain of the victims is less than the pleasure of the oppressors, but that does not justify genocide. All of this means that the greatest happiness for the greatest number is not necessarily a criterion of morality.

***

A final criticism of Bentham's hedonism is that he only takes into account the quantity of pleasure that an action offers, and he seems unconcerned with the quality of pleasure involved. That is, he does not consider that some modes of enjoyment might be qualitatively higher than others. Bentham would compare activities such as hearing a classical concert and wallowing in mud only with regard to the amount of pleasure provided by each; if the latter were more pleasurable, it would be preferred. He even went so far as to say that "quantity of pleasure being equal, pushpin [pick-up-sticks] is as good as poetry." But surely pleasures should be differentiated in terms of better and worse kinds, and not judged solely in terms of amount. The kind of pleasure seems at least as significant as degree, and might be more important altogether.

Because Bentham's utilitarianism consisted only of quantitative considerations, a reform was needed, and this was provided by his compatriot and successor John Stuart Mill According to Mill, hedonism had to take into consideration the qualitative aspect of pleasure if it was to become a doctrine respectable enough to be the goal of life. In his book *Utilitarianism*, Mill wrote, "It is quite compatible with the principle of utility to recognize the fact, that some kinds of pleasure are more desirable and more valuable than others. It would be absurd that while, in estimating all other things, quality is considered as well as quantity, the estimation of pleasures should be supposed to depend on quantity alone." Mill is here acknowledging the need for a refinement of utilitarianism.

Bentham treated animal pleasures as equal to those of human beings, and for this reason his philosophy was called "pig philosophy" (by Thomas Carlyle). The pleasures of a pig and of a person were no different in value if they were the same in amount. Bentham's concern was with more or less pleasure, not with finer or coarser pleasurers, and this implies that he would recommend to us the life of a happy pig.

The distinction that Mill has in mind can be illustrated by the following example. When we see a herd of cows or sheep grazing in a field, we might briefly feel a sense of envy, and think how marvelous it would be to lead the life of a domesticated animal, with food readily available and nothing to do but crop the grass, sleep and reproduce the species. But even though a simple existence might be momentarily appealing, we really would not want to trade places. If we had the choice, we would elect to be human even if it entailed less pleasure. We would want a higher existence, and are unimpressed by the fact that a sheep or a cow might enjoy life more.

But how are we to determine which of two pleasurable activities is qualitatively superior? What makes one pleasure higher and another lower? Mill's answer is that the better pleasure is the one chosen by the majority of people. He wrote, "Of two pleasures, if there be one to which all or almost all who have experience of both give a decided preference, irrespective of any feeling of moral obligation to prefer it, that is the more desirable pleasure."

The choices of experienced people, then, can be taken as the index of higher quality. since no knowledgeable person would ever elect a worse pleasure over a better one. As Mill noted: "no intelligent being would consent to be a fool; no instructed person would be an ignoramus, no person of feeling and conscience would be selfish and base, even though they should be persuaded that the fool, the dunce, or the rascal is better satisfied with his lot than they are with theirs." Mill went on to say, "It is better to be a human being dissatisfied than a pig satisfied; better to be a Socrates dissatisfied than a fool satisfied." The superior pleasures are the ones that engage our higher faculties.

Utilitarianism needed the addition of quality as a corrective, since the principle of the greatest happiness for the greatest number can produce a vulgar philosophy. Upon analysis, however, certain flaws appear that throw Mill's utilitarianism, and perhaps the whole of hedonism, into question.

First, to use the choices of people, as the criterion for higher pleasures does not seem reliable. People who have experienced two pleasures will not necessarily choose the higher one — however broadly one wants to define "higher." The millions of people who watch violent, bloody movies and horror shows are by and large acquainted with fine drama, but they prefer to watch what is thrilling instead. And in choosing violence they do not claim to be enjoying a higher pleasure; they simply want the lower ones. The same holds true with regard to mud wrestling compared to visiting an art gallery, a monster truck rally as compared to a dance performance. Videos featuring murder attract far more people than cultural events, but that does not show them to be more elevated. Even within the same field, the higher type of pleasure is less popular than the lower type. Better literature sells fewer copies than mass market books, classical CDs are purchased less than pop' music, and artistic films have a shorter run at the cinemas than commercial ones. In short, popular taste is not necessarily good taste, which means that, contrary to Mill's contention, the choice of the majority cannot be taken as an indication of higher quality pleasures.

Another criticism of Mill is that, as in the case of Bentham, he based his ethical views on a description of human conduct. He wrote, "The sole evidence it is possible to produce that anything is desirable, is that people do desire it.... No reason can be given why the general happiness is desirable except that each person, so far as he believes it to be attainable, desires his own happiness. This however being a fact, we have not only all the proof which the case admits of, but all which it is possible to require, that happiness is a good."

His argument is that whatever is seen is visible; whatever is heard is audible; and whatever is desired is desirable. But the term 'desirable' functions differently. What is seen must be visible or it would not be seen, and what is heard is, of course, audible, but what people desire may not be desirable; it may not be worthy of being desired, just as the desirable, may not be desired.

The alcoholic wants alcohol, and in large amounts, but that does not make it worth wanting, either for him or for society.

***

This leads us to an evaluation of happiness as the goal in living. To many ethicists, experiencing pleasure does not seem substantial enough to be the goal of human life. It seems shallow, too animalistic. People have a need to live more deeply, and to differentiate themselves from animals, to have a higher life purpose. And as we have seen, there is no necessary connection between moral conduct and actions that promote happiness, either for oneself or the majority. Even if the majority derived happiness from hanging the minority, that is no justification for it.

More importantly, Mill's concern with qualitative experience inadvertently led him to deny the primary importance of pleasure itself. Mill stated that it is better to be a dissatisfied person than a satisfied pig, or a Socrates dissatisfied rather than a fool satisfied. Here he is saying that quality of life is more valuable than enjoyment. A consistent hedonist would never approve of dissatisfaction, but Mill chose this over a life of pleasures. In this way, he subordinates the hedonistic goal of pleasure to a richer type of life — that associated with the civilized life of humans.

The general point is that when Mill, or anyone attempts to refine hedonism by introducing qualitative distinctions, they place themselves outside of hedonism altogether. The standard used to differentiate between higher and lower pleasures becomes the basic ethic, displacing pleasure as the criterion for a good life. Without realizing it, Mill ultimately took as his ethic the qualitatively better life of the more fully developed human being, abandoning hedonism and Utilitarianism altogether.

To some extent, happiness should be part of the good life. As Joseph Butler (1692–1752) commented, "when we sit down in a cool hour, we cannot justify any pursuit 'til we are convinced that it will be for our happiness, or at least not contrary to it."

But perhaps we have to look beyond hedonism for something more ultimate. Maybe we should aim at the thriving of all human dimensions — the social, aesthetic, material, emotional, political, physical, intellectual, sensuous, spiritual, and so forth, within the framework of sympathy and care for others. Our spiritual aspect might be satisfied not by worshipping a supernatural being, sitting on a heavenly throne, but by a sense of awe, majesty, and solemnity before the night sky, by the love we feel for other people, and our willingness to put their lives above our own.

Perhaps we should not look for heavenly bliss, or a choir of angels to sanctify our lives, but the realization of our potentialities, and being kind to our fellow human beings, especially those we love.

14. Nature as the Model of Existence

During the 1960s a movement spread across the nation promoting a natural way of life. It was fostered mainly by young people who wanted to live in harmony with the natural environment. They preferred the country to the city, the rhythm of the days and seasons as their measure of time, the simplicity, space, and peacefulness of the land to make them gentle, balanced, and tranquil. They wanted to eat organic food without pesticide or preservatives, to drink pure water, and breathe unpolluted air, to maintain good health through whole grain and farm-fresh foods, to do outdoor work with minimum reliance on machines. Hiking is better than driving, an open window better than air conditioning, laundry on a clothesline better than an electric dryer.

They also wanted to express themselves through crafts such as weaving, pottery, and leatherwork rather than high art, which they considered pretentious, and to dress down in ordinary clothes such as jeans and T-shirts, in natural fibers of cotton or wool, leather sandals, moccasins, or boots. Dressing up in the latest styles made you a slave to fashion. Plainness was best, simplicity, down-to-earth values. Their furniture was basic, their belongings only essentials, and plastic and synthetics were anathema. Security does not consist in what you own, but in what you can do without.

They stressed simple joys rather than sophisticated plea-sures, feeling rather than thinking, direct experience instead of knowledge gained from books. High culture was only an artifi-cial overlay, covering authentic experience. Guitars and fiddles were good, cellos and oboes, bad; square dancing and line danc-ing was real, ballroom dancing stylized and affected. Real music did not consist of concertos or symphonies, but folk and country songs drawn from the experiences of working people, and hon-est painting was not French Impressionism but naïve, primi-tive realism. They also believed in magic and astrology, Eastern faiths, and the truths revealed through hallucinogenic drugs, far outside of science and reason. Medicine should be herbal, not synthesized by pharmaceutical companies. In all things, plain-ness was best, simplicity, modesty, down-to-earth values.

The biologist E. O, Wilson postulated "biophilia" — that we need the presence of plants and animals, that we want to be close to trees, mountains, and oceans. We bring flowers to the sick to cheer them up, cultivate plants indoors, and care for fish, cats, and dogs in our homes. People leave cities on weekends and for vacations, because they need the refreshment of the woods or the water to restore their equilibrium.

This "be natural" movement favored working with your hands, farming or fishing, following trades such as carpentry, plumbing, or handyman. We should live in a wooden or stone house, not an apartment in a glass and steel high-rise, something small and functional, made of the earth's materials. A commune in the country, with shared resources, and mutual helpfulness would be best. For transportation, we should own a van or bus rather than a selfish sports car. Women's jewelry should be tur-quoise, beads, silver, and they should wear their hair long, and not try to improve on nature with cosmetics. The best sports are fishing and hunting, canoeing, white water rafting, rock climb-ing, and our children should be home-schooled, given practical skills, not abstract knowledge of history, physics, or philosophy.

***

Most likely, the "be natural" movement was precipitated by the ills of modern life — industrial pollution, unhealthy, pre-pared food, overcrowded, impersonal, noisy cities, and so forth.

But its roots can be traced far back in intellectual history, per-haps to the Greek Cynics in Athens.

The Cynics were called "the dog philosophers" by the an-cients because of their slovenly appearance. in fact, people would throw bones at them in contempt. But they were actually quite reflective and disciplined. They believed in mental control rather than physical indulgence, or conformity to social norms. They ridiculed the etiquette of Athens as over-civilized, and were unruly and shameless. defecating in public. They disdained bathing, marriage, money, and all the trappings of success, living a life of relentless poverty.

Their aim was to follow nature , which exhibits qualities of freedom, reason, and self-sufficiency. All conventions that restricted liberty must be resisted. They thought we have a re-sponsibility to oppose civil society, to disrupt its political and social restraints through outrageous behavior. Anarchy is best, because individuals can only thrive outside of government con-trol. Nothing natural is shameful, whereas civilization is evil incarnate.

The most celebrated and romantic figure among the Cynics was Diogenes, whose life spawned numerous anecdotes and leg-ends. He is reputed to have lived in a tub, his only possessions a robe, walking stick, and a bowl, and when he saw a boy eat from a lettuce leaf, then consume the leaf, and drink water from his cupped hand, he threw away his bowl as vanity and pretension. He is famous for lighting a lantern in the early morning, saying he was looking for an honest man, and when he heard that Plato had defined man as an erect, featherless biped, he plucked a bird and said "Here is Plato's man."

In one famous incident, Alexander the Great visited him as he was sunning himself in a field. "Are you not afraid of me?" Alexander asked. "Why, what are you," Diogenes responded, "a good thing or a bad thing?" "A good thing," Alexander replied. "Who then is afraid of the good?"

Alexander was so impressed that he said, "Ask anything of me that you like." Diogenes replied, "Then kindly move.out of my sunlight." As Alexander left he is reputed to have remarked, "Had I not been Alexander, I should have liked to be Diogenes."

Diogenes remains as the classic Cynic, wise, scolding, dedicated to a plain, natural life. He died at around 90, perhaps of a dog bite, or from eating raw octopus, or from holding his breath.

***

The more immediate predecessors of the naturalism movement were the Romantics of the 19th century. The American writer Henry David Thoreau is often cited in this regard, especially for his book *Walden*. "I went to the woods because I wished to live deliberately," he wrote, "to front only the essential facts of life, and see if I could not learn what it had to teach, and not, when I came time to die, discover that I had not lived. I did not wish to live what was not life, living is so dear; nor did I wish to practice resignation, unless it was quite necessary. I wanted to live deep and suck out all the marrow of life, to live so sturdily and Spartan-like as to put to rout all that was not life, to cut a broad swath and shave close, to drive life into a corner, and reduce it to its lowest terms."

Thoreau is retreating from a world that entices people to acquire more and more goods, inessential, superfluous goods, to live in debilitating comfort, and spend an excessive amount of time earning money to support a false, artificial existence. He believes that life in cities diverts people from the satisfaction of their basic needs, separates them from the beauties of nature, and the dignity of manual labor. Work should bear the stamp of our personality. Instead of self-reliance, people have become weak, dependent, and self-indulgent. Above all, cities render people oblivious to what is essential in life, whereas the demands of country living make people aware of the basic terms of existence.

The 19th century British romantic poets also found in nature the "truths" and "ideals" that they admired, and they wanted everyone to be receptive to nature's lessons. William Wordsworth, in "The Tables Turned," tells us that nature should be our teacher:

> Books! 'tis a dull and endless strife:
>
> Come, hear the woodland linnet,
>
> How sweet his music! On my life,
>
> There's more of wisdom in it...

> One impulse from a vernal wood
> May teach you more of man,
> Of moral evil and of good,
> Than all the sages can...
> Enough of Science and of Art:
> Close up those barren leaves;
> Come forth, and bring with you a heart
> That watches and receives.

Nature rather than books contains the wisdom that will nourish us, and those profound truths can only be acquired through a "wise passiveness," not by earnest effort. If we are sensitized, we can establish rapport and communion with nature. We must shed our adultness, become child-like or innocent as infants in order to understand. In "Intimations of Immortality" Wordsworth writes,

> Trailing clouds of glory do we come
> From God who is our home:
> Heaven lies about out us in our infancy!
> Shades of the prison-house begin to close
> Upon the growing Boy,
> But He beholds the light, and whence it flows,
> He sees it in his joy,
> The Youth, who daily farther from the east
> Must travel, still is Nature's Priest,
> And by the vision splendid
> Is on his way attended;
> At length the Man perceives it die away,
> And fade into the light of common day.

John Keats also celebrates nature, especially as a restorative when we are despondent. In "Endymion" he famously writes,

> A thing of beauty is a joy forever:
> Its loveliness increases; it will never
> Pass into nothingness; but still will keep

A bower quiet for us, and a sleep
Full of sweet dreams, and health, and quiet breathing...
Spite of despondence, of the inhuman dearth
Of noble natures,
Some shape of beauty moves away the pall
From our dark spirits. Such the sun, the moon,
Trees old, and young, sprouting a shady boon
For simple sheep, and such are daffodils
With the green world they live in; and clear rills
That for themselves a cooling covert make
'Gainst the hot season...
Whether there be shine, or gloom o'ercast,
They always must be with us, or we die.

***

Naturalists emphasize that we are a part of nature and should live in a harmonious relationship with our surroundings, not exploit its bounty for human benefit. But some naturalists believe we should respect nature not for our sake, but for its sake. In other words, some stress that we are reliant on nature, and if we inflict damage on it, we harm ourselves; it will rebound against us. Others believe human being have a responsibility to protect nature itself. This view is called deep ecology.

The first position points out that man is dependent on nature. We cannot live without oxygen, hydrogen and nitrogen, a habitable range of temperatures, an envelope of moisture surrounding the planet. Our atmosphere protects us from lethal ultraviolet rays, a magnetic field guards us from radiation. The sun was worshipped for centuries, and for good reason: if it weren't for its light and heat, we would not exist.

Nature provides us with the necessities of life, an environment for living. It gives us sources of energy, materials for shelter, animals and vegetables for food. Having a safe and warm home, fresh water and fertile soil, sustain our lives. Without grass and trees, the earth beneath our feet would slide and erode. Everything is interconnected in a vast ecological web.

The second view is more extreme and difficult to defend. Some naturalists believe human beings have an obligation to protect the natural environment, that it's worthy of preservation in and of itself. Not only should animals be protected from slaughter or extinction, but we have an n obligation toward trees and plants, oceans, lakes, and rivers, mountains, valleys, and deserts. We are caretakers of the land, stewards entrusted to preserve the planet. Strip mining, clear cutting, deforestation, overfishing, polluted air and water are failures in our responsibility. We are harming the Earth in ways that may not be reversible.

It is relatively easy to say we should protect the environment if we know what is good for us; we don't want an uninhabitable planet. But do animals and trees, oceans and mountains have a right to be preserved if they have no utility for people? Do we owe it to the ocean to keep it free from pollution, to keep trash from washing up on pristine, sandy beaches, and do forests have a right to grow, and not be blighted or harvested? Should rocks not be quarried, coal not to be mined, oil and gas remain underground? Rights usually imply responsibilities, and water, sand, wood, rock, and so forth have no responsibilities.

And are we accountable to animal and plant species to make sure they do not become extinct, even if this happens naturally? It is sometimes argued that we must preserve "the balance of nature," but 99% of the 4 billion species that inhabited the earth have now vanished, mainly in the "five mass extinctions." This is not man's doing but fluctuations in the heating and cooling of the planet, and changes in sea levels. Woolly mammoths and saber-tooth tigers have vanished, along with the great auk and the dodo bird. Still, we continue to have balance and diversity. Nature is resilient.

National Parks were set aside out of respect for the beauty of the landscape and as animal preserves, but also for people's enjoyment, for both preservation and recreation. And if there is a choice between building and heating our houses, or protecting trees, rocks, and oil, maybe people should have priority. Using renewable energy from the wind, the sun, biomass, thermal heat, rivers, waterfalls, and tides might be a way of avoiding that choice, but if that is not (economically) feasible, people ought to come first.

***

The environmental movement is the present manifestation of the "be natural" approach to life. We are very aware of the health of our natural surroundings — especially the welfare of animals.

Peter Singer, for example, in his book *Animal Liberation*, claims that animals are equivalent to people. They have moral standing as "sentient" beings. They have feelings, desires, memory, consciousness, and a social life. To him, regarding humans as superior is only anthropocentrism — a prejudice or bias toward members of one's own species.

Singer was once asked at a talk, "In a flood, if you could save a dog or a child, which would you choose?" He answered, "If it were an intelligent dog, and a stupid child, I would choose the dog."

Advocates of animal welfare are especially adamant about not using animals for food, that we should all convert to vegetarianism. Sometimes they use frivolous arguments such as, "Heart attacks are God's revenge for eating his furry creatures"; or "Vegetarians are kinder"; or "Since animals are our brothers, eating them is cannibalism." But there are equally silly arguments given by meat-eaters: "If God didn't want us to eat animals, he wouldn't have made them of meat" (although this is like saying, "If God didn't want us to cut down trees, he wouldn't have made them of lumber"). To the claim that vegetarians are kinder, carnivores say "It's just that aggressive people tend to be meat-eaters"; and "vegetarians don't love animals, they just hate vegetables."

A more serious argument for vegetarianism is that using animals for food is wasteful and inefficient. We must feed animals 8 pounds of protein in the form of grain, to return 1 pound of protein in the form of meat. To produce prime beef or veal, the ratio is even greater: 21:1. Some 78% of our grain goes for animal feed, which some people feel represents a wastage of 87.5%. Why not eat the grain directly? With millions of people malnourished or starving throughout the world, eating meat seems an indulgence — even if we like the taste.

More importantly, perhaps, vegetarians argue that, to meet the demand for meat, the agribusiness must rely on mass production methods factory to raise livestock — cattle, chicken, sheep, goats, and pigs. This means processing thousands of animals in ways that cause them pain. More humane methods could be used, such as free-range farming, but they are not cost-effective; if we used an open approach, only the wealthy could afford steak, veal, or bacon.

Some of the problems in factory farming are with the animals' diet, as well as in slaughtering, and shipping, but the main difficulty has to do with overcrowding. Meat and egg production is big business, and most of the animal products we eat require packing animals into small spaces. For instance, to be economically viable, chicken farmers must have a flock of thousands of birds, crowded together in small, multi-tiered, wire cages. Cramped as they are, the hens are unable stretch their wings, perch, walk, stretch, or build nests. They suffer foot damage from the wire cage, and are sometimes "debeaked" to prevent pecking injuries. Calves are confined in crates throughout their lives, and to produce "milk-fed" veal, they are not allowed exercise, or room to turn around. They spend their lives in darkness to reduce restlessness.

The American Society for the Prevention of Cruelty to Animals (A.S.P.C.A.) has said, "Daily life in factory farms is one of pain, frustration, and misery.... Factory farms pack animals into spaces so tight that most can barely move. Many have no access to the outdoors, spending their lives on open warehouse floors, or housed in cages or pens. Without the room to engage in natural behaviors, confined animals experience severe physical and mental disease."

Some naturalists even object to keeping domestic pets, which are regarded as virtual slaves. They are "owned" by their masters, whom they fawn upon, offering affection in exchange for food. Dogs and cats need to be bred down, or liberated, in the name of abolishing all forms of slavery.

The animal rights advocates are also exercised about animal testing. The Federal Food and Drug Administration requires that all new pharmaceuticals be tested before they are released to the public. The Consumer Products Safety Commission applies the same regulations to cosmetics, shampoo, hand creams, sunscreens, and so forth. The obvious reason is to protect public health. We could conduct experiments on people, but it seems preferable to use animals as "guinea pigs." We do not want carcinogenic powder or soap, much less drugs or medications.

Animal experimentation is extensive, from fruit flies, to worms, to chimpanzees. Rats and mice constitute 95% of test animals, cats and dogs less than 1%. About 100 million animals are used annually as test subjects, 10 million of which are killed in the process. We use animals for medical research into polio, smallpox, and cancer; pharmaceutical tests of toxicity and irritation; psychological experiments of conditioning, overcrowding, maternal deprivation; drug and alcohol addiction tests; and for judging the efficacy of military weapons.

To subject animals to pain, and sometimes death, seems barbaric, but it is better than causing harm to humans. Sacrificing thousands of mice is terrible, but it might be worth it to cure cancer.

Some defenders of animal welfare claim that computer simulation, or epidemiological studies can be used instead, but these methods are not as effective. Others claim there is no necessary carry-over from animals to humans, that benzene causes leukemia in people but not in mice, that aspirin is poisonous to cats. But numerous products are effective for both animals and people. We are vulnerable to over two hundred of the same health problems.

The main issue is whether we are wrong to use animals for our benefit. What makes human beings superior?

***

The be-natural theory resonates with people today, but is living naturally better than living with the advances of science and civilization? In cultural terms, good theater, dance, and films are difficult to find in the country, as are museums, galleries, and classical concert halls. People who enjoy fine architecture would be at a loss in a rural community, and those who enjoy fine food are more likely to find gourmet restaurants in major cities. Urban areas offer entertainment, from sports events, to pop' concerts, to dance clubs, and provide a wide range of stores with products that add comfort and convenience in living. There are walkable neighborhoods, public transportation, and oftentimes shorter commutes to work. Medical and dental care is better in urban areas, with more highly trained doctors and state-of-the-art hospitals, and the quality of education tends to be better in city schools. Furthermore, the population is generally more sophisticated.

Nature does provide peace, if you think of gently flowing brooks and sun-drenched meadows, but other parts of nature are savage, in a dog-eat-dog struggle for survival. The universe itself was conceived in violence, and perpetuated by it, with outbursts of supernovas, the destruction of white dwarf stars, gamma ray bursts, asteroids and comets slamming into planets.

Living in the country, close to nature can also be dull and boring, deadening people rather than enlivening them. Primitive life can reduce people to a subsistence level where they only satisfy their biological needs, and do not enjoy the more complex life of a human being. Personal development can be stifled not stimulated. And is it better to minimize material goods, or to eliminate labor-saving devices that technology has invented, to do without refrigerators or stoves or washing machines, without running water, central heating, indoor plumbing, or electric lights? Too much time would be spent on sheer survival. The farmer needs his tractor, his planting equipment, his cutter and shredder, his harvester, and all the machinery of modern agriculture to free him from exhausting, repetitive, physical labor. Having a spacious, well-decorated home can enhance our spirit far more than a log cabin or a cave, even if the cave is a more natural dwelling,

In fact, we do not know how far back we have to go in human history to reach a truly natural condition. Should we do without the wheel, or written language? Should we go without clothing, not wear shoes, eat food with our hands rather than using silverware, and must the food be raw? When we travel, must we swim across rivers or can we use bridges, and is it acceptable to drive a car or must we walk or ride a horse? Should we avoid boats, trains, and airplanes? Should we only gather fruits, nuts, and berries, or is it all right to raise livestock and grow crops? Is Neanderthal man the natural state, or must we go back to apes, amphibians, amoebas?

The minute we make changes in our natural condition, we don't know where to stop; it becomes the long-slippery-slope. We cannot claim that whatever human beings do is natural since we are a part of nature, for then it would be impossible to distinguish between the natural and the artificial. All development in science, engineering, and medicine, and the creation of culture itself would be natural.

Above all, naturalism can be criticized for assuming that nature is always good, and emulating nature is best. Some aspects of nature are beneficial to us, others are harmful. For example, eating natural foods is better than eating prepared foods with preservatives and additives, but we should not try to treat a ruptured appendix with herbal remedies. And we might want to build nature's tranquility into our lives, but not the pain, hunger, and disease that afflict all wild animals.

Furthermore, our natural environment includes tornadoes, hurricanes, earthquakes, tidal waves, volcanic eruptions, avalanches, and lightning strikes that cause forest fires, as well as jungles, desserts, swamps, and Arctic wastes. Heavy rains cause flash floods, and snowstorms cause animals to freeze to death. Bacteria, viruses, and parasites cause a host of infectious diseases such as malaria, tuberculosis, influenza, anthrax, botulism, typhus, measles, smallpox, and cancer. All of these are naturally occurring. And nature contains savage and venomous animals such as lions, panthers, tigers, alligators, and bears; sharks, box jellyfish, piranhas, and sting rays; cobras, pythons, rattlesnakes, and black mambas; and tarantulas, the brown recluse, and red and black widow spiders. There are even toxic plants such as poison ivy, oak, and sumac, as well as hemlock, nightshade, and toxic mushrooms, not to mention the insects that torment animals and carry disease.

Mother nature is not always kind, and trusting nature might not be the best course of action. We want to build a garden in the jungle, not import the jungle into our garden. Dykes, antibiotics, irrigation, serums, insecticides, etc. seem worthwhile interventions. Some aspects of nature are worth following, but others are not, just as the unnatural contains both good and bad parts. And if something can be natural but not good, then a good life is not always a natural one. We need to be selective about what we take from nature or science, in terms of what augments and what diminishes our lives.

Perhaps Francis Bacon is right in thinking that the aim of science is to restore the earth to a state close to Eden by eliminating all the evils inflicted on humanity after the Fall. Or maybe we should live in a symbiotic relationship with nature, rather than trying to master it, even though the Bible tells us otherwise. According to Genesis, God decreed we should "subdue" the earth, "have dominion over the fish of the sea, and over the fowl of the air, and over every living thing," and we have taken God at his word. But a reciprocal relationship, and cohabitation might be better.

When we look out at the night sky, we feel diminished by its depth and immensity, rendered in black and white, having nothing to do with human life. Our emotions, pleasures, pains, and loves are made pitiful by the planets and stars, wheeling in their galaxies for billions of years, compelled by physical laws. We are alien creatures, existing for a brief time, in a remote corner of the universe, struggling to find meaning in our lives. But it is unlikely we will find it in nature. The universe has no pity.

15. Rotating on Our Own Axis

Some insights into what constitutes a good life, as well as good art, are offered by the 19th century German philosopher Friedrich Nietzsche. In *The Birth of Tragedy,* he describes two forces identified with the Greek gods Apollo and Dionysus. The Apollonian represents form and reason; the Dionysian stands for passion, fueled by the thought of death. If the Apollonian predominates, then art becomes an abstraction, calcifies into a skeleton. And if the Dionysian is overpowering, then the passions cannot be organized into a coherent whole. As Marianne Moore said, it would be like playing tennis with the net down. Both are necessary forces that must be kept in a dynamic tension, for without limits, we cannot build upward, just as a preponderance of formal structure is deadening. This principle holds true in art, religion, and in civilization as a whole.

To Nietzsche, the genius of Aeschylus and Sophocles was to write plays that balanced the two. Oedipus commits patricide and incest, but the horrors are held within the framework of inevitable fate. And perhaps this is the secret of good art: an ideal blend of formal structure and emotive expression.

This carries over as a life lesson. We look back at the 19th century and see a society of rigidity and repression, endorsing whatever is suitable, appropriate, and fitting, according to custom and tradition. Our own age is characterized by emotional outpourings, in popular music and dancing, as well as in criminal violence and the armed conflict of wars. Our films, TV programs, and books feature murder, horror, and sex; our concerts, rock groups playing noisy music to frenzied audiences. We now prefer violent sports — football, boxing, hockey, and wrestling, to baseball, tennis, soccer, and golf. We choose power boats over sailboats, mountain climbing over picnics, junk food over fine cooking, video games over reading, fast cars over country walks, action over reflection. Theater, ballet, and classical concerts are declining in popularity, and opera might become outmoded altogether. Perhaps we have overshot the mark.

***

Nietzsche is part of the *existential* movement in philosophy that tries to diagnose human ills and to offer a path forward. Existentialists are concerned with the overall human condition and see certain psychological states as endemic to our existence, and philosophically important. These states must be transcended for a worthwhile life.

For instance, human beings experience a certain anxiety in living This is not the same as fear, which has an object: in fear, we are afraid of that person holding a gun, of a hurricane, or of nuclear weapons. But in anxiety we are simply apprehensive; we feel ill at ease and uncomfortable in our own skin. If we are asked what we are anxious about, we may say, "It's really nothing."

But according to the existentialists, that answer is instructive. We are anxious about nothing, the nothingness that preceded our birth and will succeed our death. We are anxious about the void, of losing consciousness, the loss of our self. In short, we are not anxious about dying, but the cessation of life. We live our lives with the consciousness that at some point, we will cease to be. There is a continual awareness of our eventual non-being, and that remains as a background to our lives. To be human, and conscious of our coming annihilation, produces never-ending anxiety.

Animals live but are not aware that they are living, much less that they will die. They gather food, groom themselves, fight, play, and mate, but are oblivious to the fact that their lives will end someday. But to be human means to know our lives are limited.

This can poison a person's existence, lead to depression and a sense of futility. It can cause denial and avoidance, a mental suicide where we seek salvation in cults. To Freud, religion is an infantile neurosis that arrests our development, so that we never fully mature. To Marx, religion is the opiate of the masses, an escape into delusions because we cannot face the reality of our death.

But the existentialists argue that we are strong enough to confront death and can use it as a catalyst to more intense living. Death adds urgency and poignancy to life, and it can make us more compassionate toward others who are facing the same fate. As Walter Pater declares in *Marius the Epicurean*, we should "burn with a hard, gem-like flame" in the time that we have, celebrating the fact that we are alive, and make the most of our brief existence.

Human beings also feel a sense of alienation, which is a gap or schism where formerly there was rapport. For one thing, we feel alienated from nature, which was our home, but we have developed to the point where living in nature is no longer comfortable. We cannot go home again, but still feel homesick. A sense of separation from other people is another form of alienation. We no longer live in small communities but in large cities, where companionship and friendship can be more difficult to form. Our children move away to places where there are job opportunities. We commute in cars that isolate us from one another in speeding compartments, and we work in cubicles in offices, or at work-stations in factories — both impersonal environments. Machines and technology also alienate us, since it is more difficult to identify with the product of our labor. Cellphones, computers, and even telephones also separate us, while claiming to facilitate communication. And for entertainment, we watch TV, everyone isolated in their private space, and going out less often to a film, concert, or sports event.

We are also alienated from God, who used to be a presence in our lives. As discussed previously, God takes a much smaller role in our thoughts and decisions today. It is as though He had withdrawn himself, abandoned humanity, leaving man to his own devices. People no longer pray for changes in the weather or praise God when a hurricane changes directions. We rely on ourselves to cope with disasters, to protect our children, and guard our health. Despair and forlornness also plague us as we realize our aloneness, with no purpose for existing, no meaning to our being.

However, the existentialists believe we can create a personal meaning for our lives, re-establish a connection with our natural roots, have greater rapport with our friends, find satisfying work, entertain ourselves in harmony with others, and so forth. We need not accept the negative dimensions of human life and can reduce our anxiety, alienation, and despair. We cannot wholly eliminate these states, because they are part of being a human being on earth, but we can oppose them, using our awareness and intelligence, and the "good angels" of our nature.

***

Perhaps we are too prone today to think there is an absence of values, or a leveling process in which everything is of equal importance, that we should withdraw and live for ourselves. But there are dimensions to our being that we can develop, leading to a gratifying life — all 7.5 billion of us.

For one thing, physical sensations are satisfying to experience: certain sights, sounds, tastes, smells, and textures, the delights of the senses. These can be experienced directly in the natural environment, or by extension in the arts and human creations. We respond to the land and landscapes, the sea and seascapes, flowers and fruit as well as still lifes, certain colors and pitches. We like the effect of sunlight filtering through leaves, and the chiaroscuro of light and dark that turns flat surfaces three dimensional. We like certain sounds, such as bird songs, light wind blowing through branches, waterfalls, children's shouts at play, as well as a cello or guitar, a piano, the white sound of a flute, and the human voice singing. Some melodies and harmonies are lovely to hear.

We also respond to certain textures — silk, moss, marble, bark, and the smell of flowers, perfumes, spices, the aroma of food. And we like the taste of nuts, and berries, fruits, vegetables, and meat. Fine cooking is an art, and we relish a well-cooked meal with a complex blend of flavors.

The pleasures of the senses lead us to sensuality, especially sexual desire and satisfaction. Sex can rule our lives, or serve as an enhancement. We are flesh and blood creatures, after all, and have bodily needs that can be condemned but not denied.

We also want the physical pleasure of sports, where we compete against others on the field or on a court, enjoying the testing of our skills. The ancient Greeks in particular valued athletic competition as "physical training for health", as an accompaniment to mental education. The Latin phrase is *mens sana in corpore sano*, a sound mind in a healthy body.

Greek athletes competed in the Olympic Games, a religious event held in honor of Zeus, and the victors were honored for their abilities and passion, a wreath of olive leaves placed around their head as a sign of excellence. For almost twelve centuries the Games drew athletes and spectators from across the Hellenic world, featuring chariot racing, discus throwing, hurling the javelin, boxing, and wrestling. The competition also had a military flavor, training citizens for war, but displacing aggression in a non-harmful way. In general, athletics was valued by the Greeks as "a way of communicating, that brings a great sense of connection between people."

Our emotions are also an important part of human life, feelings of joy, despair, desire, sadness, fear, grief. And relationships engage our emotions most fully, especially friendships and love relationships, where we are at one with another person. We know that living two-by-two, and being part of a family, is preferable to a solitary life. We are social creatures, and hermits are few and far between. Loving and being loved is deeply fulfilling, and one of our greatest adventures.

Husbands, wives, children, and partners evoke strong feelings of caring, protectiveness, joy, and affection. A family can be experienced as warmth and security, a bulwark against an impersonal world. So can being part of a community, which gives us a sense of belonging to humankind. And to quiet our emotions, we turn to the woods or meadows. A thunderstorm will unsettle us; the presence of animals, reassures us.

We are also intellectual creatures, and the life of the mind is a significant part of us, something unique to humans — at least in its higher functioning. We not only live, but reflect on our lives, and consider issues raised by the experience of living. We are creatures who want to know, as Aristotle said, and are curious about the cosmos, and where we fit in the scheme of things. We wonder whether our nature is formed by biology, society, economics, and politics, or whether we have the freedom to form ourselves. Physicists, mathematicians, and philosophers specu-late at the fringes of knowledge, representatives of the cerebral life.

We are also creative creatures who want to express ourselves imaginatively. Painting makes us see better, music to hear bet-ter, and we know what we are thinking when we write it down. Children want to scribble with crayons, build sand castles, play a wind or string instrument, be on stage in the school play. We all manifest creativity, even in our daily lives, and we are respon-sive to the arts when we encounter them, if it is good art, feeling enchanted and elevated above common life.

In addition, we are moral creatures, and that part of us should be realized as well. We feel sympathy for people who are in pain and want to alleviate their suffering, even if we derive nothing from it. Cynics say we hope for reciprocity when we are suffering, but it seems a spontaneous response, not a premedi-tated, self-serving act. Even animals help one another, dolphins carrying a wounded dolphin to the surface to breathe, and chim-panzees bringing food to a sick member of the group. Human beings too have a sense of pity, and seem impelled to care for one another. We realize that we are our brother's keeper. Maybe that is what is meant by our spiritual part, and our conscience is our soul.

Following our best aspects can lead to a fulfilling life. We ex-perience a satisfaction that has nothing to do with a preordained purpose. Actualizing the essential parts of our nature while re-taining our lucidity and compassion can produce something worthwhile. No one wants to live in a society with an anarchy of values, where people have no direction or sense of shame. Lucki-ly, we do not have to. Without being deluded, and without hurt-ing others, we can achieve an exaltation in living.

Printed in the United States
by Baker & Taylor Publisher Services